PALEO SLOW COOKER

The Ultimate Guide of Slow Cooker Cooking

(The Easiest Ways to Cook Paleo Recipes)

Angelo Kane

Published by Sharon Lohan

© Angelo Kane

All Rights Reserved

Paleo Slow Cooker: The Ultimate Guide of Slow Cooker Cooking (The Easiest Ways to Cook Paleo Recipes)

ISBN 978-1-990334-08-5

All rights reserved. No part of this guide may be reproduced in any form without permission in writing from the publisher except in the case of brief quotations embodied in critical articles or reviews.

Legal & Disclaimer

The information contained in this book is not designed to replace or take the place of any form of medicine or professional medical advice. The information in this book has been provided for educational and entertainment purposes only.

The information contained in this book has been compiled from sources deemed reliable, and it is accurate to the best of the Author's knowledge; however, the Author cannot guarantee its accuracy and validity and cannot be held liable for any errors or omissions. Changes are periodically made to this book. You must consult your doctor or get professional medical advice before using any of the suggested remedies, techniques, or information in this book.

Table of contents

Part 1 1
Introduction 2
Chapter 1: What Exactly is the Paleo Diet? 3
Chapter 2: The Origins of the Paleo Diet 8
Chapter 3: Proper Foods to Eat 13
Chapter 4: Foods to Avoid 17
Chapter 5: Parting Remarks 22
Breakfast 23
Frittata 23
Kale Casserole 24
Mexican Casserole 25
Pumpkin Pie Breakfast Sorghum 26
Butternut Squash Oatmeal 27
Cashew Porridge 28
Amaranth Apple Breakfast Pudding 29
Breakfast Casserole 30
Eggs, Chorizo and Squash 31
Egg Casserole 33
Lunch 34
Pulled Chicken Wraps 34
Mediterranean Eggplant Salad 35
Paleo Chicken Soup 36

Cauliflower Bacon Soup 37
Egg Roll Soup 38
Sausage Kale Soup 39
Butternut Squash Soup 40
Curry Pumpkin Soup 41
Vegetable Korma 43
Chicken Soup 45
Dinner 47
Sweet Short Ribs with Ginger 47
Balsamic Blackberry Chicken 47
Slow-Cooked Beef with Root Veggies and Kale 49
Slow Cooker Chicken Chili 50
Perfect Slow Cooker Roast Chicken 51
Simple Beef Stew 53
Lamb Stew 55
Chicken Curry 56
Carnitas Lettuce Wraps with Pineapple and Salsa .. 57
Chicken Ropa Vieja 59
Country Cooking Slow Cooker Neck Bones 61
Lemon Chicken 61
Honey-Dijon Chicken 63
Slow Cooker Bacon and Chicken 64
Butter Chicken 65
Ratatouille 67

Roasted Chicken	69
Sausage and Peppers	70
Pork with Kale	71
Balsamic Beef	73
Slow Cooked Turkey Breasts	74
Spicy Chicken Taco Meat	74
Rotisserie Chicken	76
Whole Chicken in the Slow Cooker	77
Slow Cooked Chicken Thighs	78
Slow Cooker Brisket with Onions	79
Thai Chicken Breasts	81
Leg of Lamb with Parsnips	81
Slow Cooker Italian Chicken	83
Fiesta Chicken	84
Slow Cooker Ham	85
Slow Cooker Meatballs	85
Braised Short Ribs	86
Shredded Beef Tacos	88
Kielbasa and Cabbage	89
Butter Chicken	90
Moroccan Chicken	91
Lemon Garlic Chicken	92
Pineapple-Cranberry Pork Loin	93
Crispy Slow Cooker Turkey	95

Balsamic Chicken 95
Slow Cooker Kalua Pork.. 96
Apricot Slow Cooker Chicken 98
Shredded Puttanesca Chicken 99
Sticky Honey Pecan Chicken 100
Pulled BBQ Chicken.. 101
Ranchero Chicken 103
Mediterranean Salmon 104
Pork and Squash Ragout 105
Chipotle Pumpkin Chicken.. 106
Brussel Sprouts with Bacon and Chicken 107
Shredded Taco Meat 108
Pineapple Pork Ribs 109
Paleo Turkey Meatballs 110
BBQ Pork Spare Ribs 111
Persian Lamb and Eggplant Stew.................................... 112
Chicken with Tomatoes 113
Spicy Beef Curry Stew 114
Cuban Chicken... 115
Middle Eastern Ribs.. 117
Mongolian Beef 118
Korean Short Ribs... 119
Moroccan Chicken 120
Lemon Dill Halibut.. 121

Honey-Poached Salmon	122
Veggie Spaghetti	123
Spicy Ginger Lime Wings	124
Squash and Ground Beef Curry	125
Easy Sausage Casserole	127
Chicken Tikka Masala	127
Pork Ribs in Spicy Adobo Sauce	129
Tuscan Chicken	130
Mushroom Chicken	131
Sweet and Spicy Chicken Legs	133
Desserts & Snacks	134
Unsweetened Pear Applesauce	134
Classic Homemade Applesauce	135
Apple-Cranberry Dessert	136
Cinnamon Poached Pears	137
Pumpkin Butter	138
Stuffed Apples	139
Power Bars	140
Part 2	142
Introduction	143
Eggs and Breakfast	145
Veggie Spinach Omelette	145
Butternut Squash N'Oatmeal	146
Paleo Mexican Breakfast Casserole	147

Mexican Casserole 148
Apple Cinnamon Oatmeal.. 149
Blueberry Oatmeal 150
Apple Quinoa with Cinnamon... 152
Chicken 153
Curry Chicken 153
Polynesian Chicken 154
Balsamic Mushroom and Chicken..................................... 155
Healthy Chicken Yakitori 156
Tasty Chicken Fillets... 157
Southwest Chicken 159
Honey Chicken 161
Chicken Broths 162
Beef... 163
Salsa Verde Beef 163
Beef Machaca 164
Balsamic Beef... 165
Chorizo Spiced Pulled Beef 166
Beef with Vegetables 167
Beef with Vegetables 169
Beef with Broccoli... 170
Mushrooms... 171
Herb Mushrooms 171
Potato with Mushrooms.. 173

Rosemary Mushrooms 174
Soups and Stews 175
Pumpkin Soup 175
Fiesta Chicken Stew 176
Chicken Soup.. 178
Cream of Chicken and Rice Soup 179
Beef and Pepper Stew 181
Spinach Chicken Soup 182
Pumpkin Chicken Soup.. 184
Beef and Vegetables Stew... 185

Part 1

Introduction

So, you want to get started on the Paleo diet? Very nice decision! This book is here to help you get acquainted with the diet and to aid you as you venture forth in a possibly life changing experience.

Like all diets, the Paleo diet will not be a simple one to follow at first, but after you understand some of the ins and outs of the diet, it will become second-nature to you. It's not one of the phony "cure-all" diets you see on television or in magazine ads. It's hard to compare the Paleo diet with other diets out there simply because it's more of a lifestyle than a modern-day diet. Nevertheless, this diet and lifestyle change is a tough undertaking and will require patience and plenty of self-discipline (trust me, if you think that donut is tempting now, it will be like the forbidden fruit once you start the Paleo diet). Everyone can reap the benefits of this lifestyle change if they put in the effort.

Chapter 1: What Exactly is the Paleo Diet?

In short, the entire purpose of the Paleo diet is to revert our eating habits back to our ancestors' way of eating — in that, you'll focus your eating habits around what our cavemen ancestors ate. Now, that doesn't mean you must invent the time machine and hunt mammoths! It simply means that a lot of the foods we eat today — foods that were not available to our cavemen ancestors — are off the table (no pun intended).

A lot of your "typical" diets include something about not eating sugars or fats or processed foods. While all of these shouldn't be indulged in every day, it's not as simple as cutting the fat off your steak for dinner. However, anything processed is definitely off limits (which means most things packed with preservatives, anything that requires a lot of processing to create, and of course all those sugary sweets).

So, what does that leave you to eat, aspiring Paleo dieters? Well, think back to the days of hunting and gathering. If you keep that in mind, you'll have an easy little cheat sheet to help you remember what you can eat while abiding by the Paleo lifestyle: Anything that our ancestors could have hunted or gathered.

This basically narrows your food down to two large groups of foods: food you could hunt and food you could gather (after all, your ancestors *were* hunter-gatherers). While this may seem limiting when you think about all the different foods you won't be able to enjoy any longer, the Paleo diet is actually far less limiting than, say, any other calorie-counting diet plan.

You may be wondering how exactly that's possible. Well, the Paleo diet does not place an emphasis on calorie intake (as many diets do), but rather focuses on the type of food that one ingests. The Paleo diet limits the food you eat (and therefore your caloric intake) to foods that are attainable through those two methods I mentioned earlier: Hunting and gathering. As you can imagine, many foods with an excessively high calorie count probably aren't found in nature – you're not going to find a sugar-laden chocolate bar roaming around in the woods!

Limiting the food you eat to these naturally occurring plants and animals will naturally limit the amount of calories you ingest in a given day, which means another piece of good news for you: No more calorie calculations or counting, unless you're inclined to do so! Put your notebooks and smartphone apps away. The Paleo diet is designed to, essentially, count calories for you so you don't have to even think about it. After all, why should you worry about the exact amount of energy you put in your body if you know you're eating healthy and natural foods? For those who are interested, though, this book has comprehensive nutritional information for each recipe, which will be helpful if you're targeting certain macronutrient ratios.

At this point, there are usually one or two people that become skeptical of the Paleo diet and its seemingly easy set of rules. The Paleo diet is a very legitimate diet and, like any other diet out there, is not that easy.

Don't be worried about the difficulty of the diet. All diets require dedication, a bit of effort, and some time before the benefits start to show, but the Paleo diet is designed in order to make it as simple as possible: just follow the healthy rules it provides, and watch both losing weight and maintaining a healthy body become as easy as pie!

The next question that might be on your mind is something along the lines of "haven't humans evolved since our cavemen ancestors? How do we stay as fit as them if I can pick up three boxes of packaged frozen dinners from the store down the street?" While it's true that we are biologically different from our ancestors to some degree, it's equally as true that our ancestors didn't have the luxury of stores to drive to and pick up pounds and pounds of food. Nor did they have packaged frozen dinners, so avoid those as well.

Our ancestors relied on going out into the wild and finding food to survive. Mix their constant exercise that came from physically searching for their next meal with their diet consisting of all-natural meats and fruits, and you've got one healthy lifestyle.

This doesn't mean you should go out and hunt deer in the park a few blocks away with nothing but your hand-whittled spear and a loin cloth, but it does mean you should focus on getting mild to average levels of exercise throughout your week while watching the food you eat. Like I said, the Paleo diet is like many other diets in a lot of ways, but easier.

Chapter 2: The Origins of the Paleo Diet

What's this? A history lesson in a Paleo book? You better believe it! It's important to know a brief history of the diet before diving in head first. Understanding where, why, and how the Paleo diet started may not be necessary information to you, but it can explain the science behind it and why it became so popular, for all the skeptics out there.

Surprisingly, and arguably, the idea of a diet revolving around our Paleolithic ancestors was inspired by the works of Charles Darwin and his theorizing of how evolution works. Evolutionarily speaking, we humans (both as cavemen and as their modern counterparts) are designed to live a certain way to maintain peak health. Think about it – when we first discovered fire, do you think we would have survived long if all we ate was fast food? Probably not.

Rather, as evolution suggests, the fittest will survive in the long run. While this doesn't mean whoever is physically fit will survive (the notion of "fitness" has more to do with adaptability in the context of evolutionary science), our ancestors would not have fared well if they were as overweight as many individuals are today.

Lucky for us, we don't need to constantly chase our food (or run from the threat of being something else's food) thanks to advancements in technology and science. We lead pretty cushy lives, and because of that we don't need to stay in top physical shape to avoid being eaten or killed.

So, diets were created and tested in order to maintain a healthy lifestyle alongside an increasingly sedentary way of life. Some worked alright, others didn't provide any results. In the mid-1980s, however, more and more nutritionists started writing about the ways our cavemen ancestors found and ate food, and how their diets differed from our own. Those nutritionists noticed a lack of several types of food (which we consider staple food today) and put it to reason that our lack of overall healthiness derives less from a lack of exercise (although it doesn't help) and more from an increase in certain foods we ingest.

Many people concluded that stable farming has a lot to do with the change in humanity's collective biological differences between us and our ancestors. With farming comes one type of food that plays a significant role in how our body interacts with foods and how we utilize the energy we ingest: carbohydrates. Before farming, humans had no way of storing and eating copious quantities of carb-heavy foods. This change is one of the most major differences between humanity then and humanity now. We'll talk more about carbohydrates in a later section.

Anyhow, skip ahead to 2007. For several decades, people have gone on TV and tried to sell easy cures to obesity and one-step weight loss programs. People were desperate for a diet or lifestyle to help them stay in shape. Quickly, and seemingly out of nowhere, people begin to talk about these papers from nearly twenty years prior – papers about the Paleolithic diet and the differences between our diet and the diets of our ancestors. Groups of individuals put the theory to the test and started to rely on more natural foods (like those of our ancestors) and noticed drastic changes to their body weight, their energy levels, and their overall health. These changes came as a shock because, despite the drastic increase in health, those individuals didn't need to put in a lot of the effort as they did with the other diets they had tried. In fact, it almost came naturally to many of them.

Finally, skip ahead to 2014. The Paleo diet has spiked in popularity and people can't get enough. Large sample sizes of hundreds of thousands of people have shown that the diet offers generally positive results with relatively minimal effort. Those who thought the diet was another hipster fad are seeing the benefits on a large scale, scientists are looking into the chemical changes in the body that come about due to the diet, and people are beginning to take the diet seriously.

Like tons of different things in the world, the Paleo diet started out as a small niche of people trying something new. This small group who tested the Paleo diet noticed results and went on to tell others about it.

Papers were published, scientific studies were performed, and people all over the world began to see the benefits of the diet.

Chapter 3: Proper Foods to Eat

The Paleo diet does have a fairly strict list of foods you can and cannot eat, but the list of foods that you *are* able to eat contains so many foods that you may not even realize there are rules in place. The Paleo diet, while avoiding foods most people are willing to declare unhealthy (frozen and preservative-filled foods), also works more to educate you on how much unnecessary processing goes into everyday foods and how you can avoid ingesting too many processed ingredients.

Meats are a wonderful way to get protein and fats for energy without having to rely on sugars or carbs (we'll get into how bad carbs can sometimes be in the next section). When many people think "meat," they may easily first jump to the image of frozen chicken nuggets in a bag. These are not good! These are processed and should be avoided.

What the general Paleo diet doctrine suggests is high-quality hormone-free meats, just like the meats you (or your cavemen ancestors) would find out in the wild grazing naturally. These meats are not bulked up with steroids and live a relatively healthy life before being eaten. Buying raw meat (whether you buy it from the butcher or buy it straight from the farm) allows you to monitor every step of its preparation and cooking so that you know there are no preservatives or other mysterious steps involved.

Back in the old days, our ancestors could find a wide variety of meats, such as red meats from cows, white meats from turkeys and chickens, and fish from rivers. Just like the cavemen, you are not limited to eating only one kind of meat, and you shouldn't completely avoid red meat by any means. Rather, focus on the quality of the meat and where the meat comes from.

As our ancestors were also gatherers, fruits and vegetables were a huge part of their diets as well. Fruits and berries would be picked fresh from the vine and eaten as they were. If you go apple picking in the fall, you are participating in the exact same steps to collecting your food. Fruits should be typically eaten raw for their full benefits, but that doesn't mean don't be creative.

Vegetables are much more versatile and many require cooking or steaming before they can be fully enjoyed. Like meats, there are a lot of farms out there that rely on chemicals and steroids to produce the "best" veggies they can. While these may not be the worst things to put into your body, organic vegetables should always be your first choice when shopping.

Better yet, one way you know our ancestors would have eaten something is if you can grow it yourself. Anything you can grow in your backyard (aside from grains) will make a perfect addition to the Paleo diet. While our ancestors didn't have farming, growing fruits and vegetables is the closest you will come to finding a stalk of broccoli in the wild if you live in the suburbs.

Foods that you should definitely eat while on the Paleo diet:

1. Fruits
2. Oils and fats
3. Vegetables (cooked or raw, it's up to you!)
4. Meats (as additive- and chemical-free as you can find)

5. Nuts and seeds
6. Seafood

Chapter 4: Foods to Avoid

Back in the days of hunting and gathering, our ancestors relied on only the foods that they could, well, hunt and gather. Humans had not discovered the ease of farming yet, so all of their food was seasonal and in small number. Because there was no farming to take advantage of, our ancestors lacked one food that people tend to overeat in the modern world: grains.

That's right, no oats, no pasta, no quinoa, and no cereal. Whereas meats contain mostly proteins and (healthy) fats, and fruits contain natural sugars and a whole slew of vitamins, grains consist mostly of things called carbohydrates, which do not interact well with our body.

While those proteins and fats from meat products build our muscles and give us fast-burning energy respectively, and the vitamins from fruit help to balance the chemicals in our bodies, the carbohydrates in grains become slower-burning sugars when we ingest them. While this sounds like it could be helpful for long-term activities, and some will argue that it definitely is, those slow-burning sugars are converted to fat if not used, which is then stored in the body for when it needs to burn off a little excess energy. If you weren't going to eat for a day or two after eating a large bowl of spaghetti, that extra fat may be alright, but if you plan on enjoying a meal or two the following day, you would just be placing more energy to burn over the fat, so that extra fat (and the extra inch around your waist) won't be burned off, and will in fact stick around for a while.

In short, avoid grains while following the Paleo diet.

One food group that many Paleo dieters tend to be on the fence about is dairy. While milk is technically found in nature, it's a bit odd that humans drink other animals' milk, isn't it? Milk is created within animal bodies in order to provide sustenance for that creature's young, whether we're talking about humans, cats, or *any* mammal.

Typically, in the animal kingdom, older siblings and adults are lactose intolerant to milk from any source.

This evolutionary trait allows younger siblings, who can't go out and find food on their own, to drink their mother's milk. Humans have forcibly ignored this natural progression and forced ourselves to continue to drink milk after we've long stopped needed our own mother's milk.

Humans are weird for this, but it's normal within society. In short, drinking milk (from any animal) is up to you as an individual, but it should never be a common drink of choice because of how dense it is in calories.

Processed foods are foods that every dietician and high school health teacher will tell you to avoid – and for good reason! Processed foods tend to be high in fat and sugars. All the negatives aside, you know for a fact that our ancestors couldn't have gone to the closest grocery store and picked up a bag of processed burritos.

Processed foods are tricky because they are everywhere in the world today. Ninety-nine percent of the foods in the freezer section are processed to some degree. All snack foods, chips, pre-packaged cookies, and fast food are also almost entirely made from processed foods with elevated levels of corn syrup. It's hard to avoid processed foods in the modern world, but that's all the more reason to do so.

Our cavemen ancestors didn't have the methods to produce processed foods and high concentrations of corn syrup, so avoid those at all costs!

One uncomplicated way to track what may be processed (and therefore less natural, and *therefore* less healthy) is to check the shelf life. Typically, the longer the shelf life, the more processing the food underwent or the more preservatives in the food itself (preservatives should also be avoided), which means it's a food that our ancestors wouldn't have had access to.

Of course, there are exceptions. Some foods have naturally longer shelf lives than others (honey, for example, doesn't go bad despite being all natural). It's best to research foods before grabbing them in bulk anyways.

For those who just want to see a quick list, here's a quick list of foods you should avoid:

1. Legumes (including peanuts)
2. All types of grains (including cereals, rice, wheat and bread)
3. White potatoes
4. Dairy products
5. Highly-processed foods
6. Refined sugars (which is also found in corn syrup)

Chapter 5: Parting Remarks

Now you know some of the basics of the Paleo diet and the foods that our ancestors ate to stay as healthy as they were. It's now up to you to decide if you want to move forward with this exciting new lifestyle, or try another option. This diet may not be for every single person out there, but remember all diets take work and self-discipline, so be prepared to struggle through temptation and be healthier for it.

Let's now get into the recipes!

Enjoy!

Breakfast

Frittata

Prep Time: 10 minutes; Cook Time: 2-3 hours
Serving Size: **101g;** Serves: **8**; Calories: **120**
Total Fat: **7.9g** Saturated Fat: **2.8g;** Trans Fat: **0g**
Protein: **8.4g;** Net Carbs: **2.7g**
Total Carbs: **3.7g;** Dietary Fiber: **1g**; Sugars: **2.3g**
Cholesterol: 192mg; Sodium: 189mg; Potassium: 165mg;
Vitamin A: 63%; **Vitamin C**: 73%; **Calcium**: 6%; **Iron**: 8%.

Ingredients:
- ¾ cups spinach, frozen
- 1 ½ cups diced red bell pepper
- ¼ cups diced red onion
- 8 eggs, beaten
- 1 teaspoon sea salt
- 1⅓ cups cooked sausage

Directions:
1. Place the frozen spinach, diced red pepper, diced onions, eggs, salt and sausage in a well-greased slow cooker.
2. Cook on low for 2 to 3 hours or until the frittata is set.

Kale Casserole

Prep Time: **10 minutes;** Cook Time: **6 hours**
Serving Size: **112g;** Serves: **8**; Calories: **185**
Total Fat: **10.1g** Saturated Fat: **5.4g;** Trans Fat: **0g**
Protein: **9.8g;** Net Carbs: **12.6g**
Total Carbs: **14g;** Dietary Fiber: **1.4g;** Sugars: **1.8g**
Cholesterol: 200mg; Sodium: 210mg; Potassium: 213mg;
Vitamin A: 40%; **Vitamin C**: 23%; **Calcium**: 7%; **Iron**: 11%.

Ingredients:
- 2 tablespoons coconut oil
- 1⅓ cups sliced leeks
- 1 cup chopped kale
- 8 large eggs
- ⅔ cups grated sweet potato
- 1 ½ cups sliced beef sausage

Directions:
1. Heat the coconut oil in a skillet. Toss in the leeks and kale and sauté for 3 to 5 minutes.
2. In a separate bowl, combine the eggs, sweet potato, beef sausage and the sautéed vegetables.
3. Pour everything into a slow cooker and cook for 6 hours on low.

Mexican Casserole

Prep Time: 10 minutes; Cook Time: 6-8 hours
Serving Size: **293g**; Serves: **4**; Calories: **340**
Total Fat: **21.2g** Saturated Fat: **6.2g**; Trans Fat: **0g**
Protein: **23.4g**; Net Carbs: **11.6g**
Total Carbs: **14.4g**; Dietary Fiber: **2.8g**; Sugars: **7.7g**
Cholesterol: 423mg; Sodium: 839mg; Potassium: 688mg;
Vitamin A: 13%; **Vitamin C**: 100%; **Calcium**: 9%; **Iron**: 26%.

Ingredients:
- 1 sweet potato, cubed
- 8 eggs, whisked
- ½ pound turkey bacon
- 1 yellow onion, chopped
- 1 red bell pepper, chopped
- 8 ounces mushrooms, chopped
- ½ packet taco seasoning

Directions:
1. Fry the bacon in a skillet. Set aside, let it chill and crumble it to pieces.
2. Toss the onion into the same skillet and sauté until translucent.
3. Place the bacon, eggs, sautéed onions, sweet potato, pepper, mushrooms and seasoning into the slow cooker. Stir well.

4. Cook for 6 to 8 hours on low.

Pumpkin Pie Breakfast Sorghum

Prep Time: **10 minutes**; Cook Time: **8 hours**
Serving Size: **163g**; Serves: **4**; Calories: **215**
Total Fat: **2.2g** Saturated Fat: **0.2g**; Trans Fat: **0g**
Protein: **6.4g**; Net Carbs: **42.5g**
Total Carbs: **46.9g**; Dietary Fiber: **4.4g**; Sugars: **7.5g**
Cholesterol: **0mg**; Sodium: **45mg**; Potassium: **228mg**;
Vitamin A: 107%; **Vitamin C**: 3%; **Calcium**: 15%; **Iron**: 15%.

Ingredients:
- 1 cup sorghum, rinsed
- 1 cup unsweetened almond milk
- ¾ cup pumpkin purée
- 2 tablespoons maple syrup
- 1 teaspoon pumpkin pie spice

Directions:
1. Combine all the ingredients and 2 cups of water in a slow cooker. Stir, cover with a lid and cook on low for 8 hours, until all the liquid is absorbed.

Butternut Squash Oatmeal

Prep Time: **10 minutes**; Cook Time: **8 hours**
Serving Size: **220g;** Serves: **4**; Calories: **272**
Total Fat: **19.8g** Saturated Fat: **2.6g;** Trans Fat: **0g**
Protein: **6.5g;** Net Carbs: **15g**
Total Carbs: **22.6g;** Dietary Fiber: **7.6g**; Sugars: **10.5g**
Cholesterol: 0mg; Sodium: 123mg; Potassium: 449mg; **Vitamin A**: 117%; **Vitamin C**: 41%; **Calcium**: 11%; **Iron**: 38%.

Ingredients:
- ½ cup raw walnuts
- ½ cup raw almonds
- 1 medium butternut squash, peeled and cubed
- 1 teaspoon cinnamon
- 2 apples, peeled and cubed
- 1 cup coconut milk

Directions:
1. Soak the walnuts and almonds in water for 12 hours.
2. Rinse the nuts and blend them in a food processor to a flour-like consistency.
3. Place the nut meal, butternut squash, cinnamon, apples and coconut milk into the slow cooker.
4. Cook for 8 hours on low.
5. When done, mash with a potato masher to your desired consistency.
6. Top with currants, coconut or maple syrup.

Cashew Porridge

Prep Time: **10 minutes;** Cook Time: **1 hour**
Serving Size: **61g;** Serves: **4**; Calories: **373**
Total Fat: **33.3g** Saturated Fat: **11.9g**; Trans Fat: **0g**
Protein: **8g**; Net Carbs: **10.4g**
Total Carbs: **14.4g**; Dietary Fiber: **4g**; Sugars: **5.2g**
Cholesterol: **0mg;** Sodium: **9mg;** Potassium: **73mg;**
Vitamin A: 0%; **Vitamin C**: 0%; **Calcium**: 3%; **Iron**: 18%.

Ingredients:
- ½ cup raw unsalted cashews
- ¼ cup pumpkin seeds, shelled
- ½ cup pecan halves
- ½ cup unsweetened dried coconut shreds
- 2 teaspoon coconut oil, melted
- 1 tablespoon maple syrup
- 1 cup water

Directions:
1. Combine all the ingredients, except for water, coconut oil and maple syrup, in a blender and blend for 30 seconds.
2. Place all the ingredients, including the oil, maple syrup and water in a slow cooker and cook on high for 1 hour. Serve immediately.

Amaranth Apple Breakfast Pudding

Prep Time: **10 minutes**; Cook Time: **8 hours**
Serving Size: **172g**; Serves: **8**; Calories: **302**
Total Fat: **8.6g** Saturated Fat: **4.9g**; Trans Fat: **0g**
Protein: **7.6g**; Net Carbs: **44.2g**
Total Carbs: **51.8g**; Dietary Fiber: **7.6g**; Sugars: **15.3g**
Cholesterol: **0mg**; Sodium: **11mg**; Potassium: **361mg**;
Vitamin A: 1%; **Vitamin C**: 31%; **Calcium**: 9%; **Iron**: 52%.

Ingredients:
- 2 cups amaranth
- ¼ cup shredded coconut
- 1/3 cup chopped walnuts
- ½ cup raisins
- 2 tablespoons coconut oil
- 2 ½ cups water
- 1 cup coconut milk
- 4 small apples, chopped
- 1 teaspoon cinnamon
- 1 tablespoon vanilla extract

Directions:
1. Place all the ingredients into the slow cooker and cook on low for 8 hours.

Breakfast Casserole

Prep Time: 10 minutes; Cook Time: 6-8 hours
Serving Size: **245g;** Serves: **6**; Calories: **249**
Total Fat: **12.9g** Saturated Fat: **4.7g;** Trans Fat: **0g**
Protein: **15.6g;** Net Carbs: **14.3g**
Total Carbs: **17.2g;** Dietary Fiber: **2.9g**; Sugars: **2.8g**
Cholesterol: 379mg; Sodium: 212mg; Potassium: 547mg;
Vitamin A: 14%; **Vitamin C**: 64%; **Calcium**: 9%; **Iron**: 16%.

Ingredients:
- 1 onion, diced
- 2 garlic cloves, minced
- 4 sausages, casing removed
- 2 cups shredded sweet potatoes
- 1 bell pepper, diced
- 8 button mushrooms, sliced
- 12 eggs
- 1 cup full-fat coconut milk
- 1 green onion, sliced

Directions:
1. Grease a skillet and sauté the onion and minced garlic for 1 to 2 minutes.
2. Toss in the sausages and break them apart while cooking for about 6 minutes.

3. Put the sweet potatoes into the slow cooker and top it with the sausages.
4. Add the diced pepper and mushrooms.
5. In a separate bowl, whisk the eggs and coconut milk. Pour the egg mixture on top of the sausages.
6. Cover with a lid and cook on low for 6 to 8 hours.
7. When done, serve topped with sliced green onions.

Eggs, Chorizo and Squash

Prep Time: 20 minutes; Cook Time: 6-8 hours
Serving Size: **268g;** Serves: **6**; Calories: **515**
Total Fat: **39.1g** Saturated Fat: **14.7g**; Trans Fat: **0g**
Protein: **31.2g**; Net Carbs: **6.3g**
Total Carbs: **7.9g**; Dietary Fiber: **1.6g**; Sugars: **3g**
Cholesterol: 438mg; Sodium: 1070mg; Potassium: 572mg;
Vitamin A: 14%; **Vitamin C**: 17%; **Calcium**: 9%; **Iron**: 23%.

Ingredients:
- 1 small butternut squash
- coconut oil, for greasing
- 1 onion, diced
- 2 cloves garlic, minced
- 1 pound Chorizo sausage
- 12 large eggs
- 1 cup coconut milk

Directions:
1. Peel and dice the squash.

2. Warm the coconut oil in a skillet and toss in the onion and garlic. Sauté for a few minutes, then add the Chorizo sausage.
3. In a small bowl, whisk together the eggs and coconut milk.
4. Grease the slow cooker and layer the squash on the bottom. Then add the Chorizo and pour over the egg mixture.
5. Cook on low for 6 to 8 hours.

Egg Casserole

Prep Time: 20 minutes; Cook Time: 8-10 hours
Serving Size: **220g**; Serves: **8**; Calories: **467**
Total Fat: **35.5g** Saturated Fat: **15.2g**; Trans Fat: **0g**
Protein: **23.4g**; Net Carbs: **7.4g**
Total Carbs: **9.1g**; Dietary Fiber: **1.7g**; Sugars: **4.1g**
Cholesterol: 322mg; Sodium: 1112mg; Potassium: 294mg;
Vitamin A: 12%; **Vitamin C**: 55%; **Calcium**: 6%; **Iron**: 16%.

Ingredients:
- 1 pound bacon, cooked and chopped
- 1 tablespoon coconut oil
- 1 red onion, diced
- 1 bell pepper, diced
- 2 cloves garlic, minced
- 2 medium yams, grated
- 12 eggs
- 1 cup coconut milk
- 1 teaspoon dill

Directions:
1. Grease the slow cooker.
2. Heat the coconut oil in a skillet and sauté the onion, garlic and bell pepper for 2 to 3 minutes.

3. In the slow cooker, layer 1/3 of the grated yams, 1/3 of the onion mixture and 1/3 of the bacon. Repeat two more times.
4. In a small bowl, whisk together the eggs, coconut milk and dill. Pour the mixture over the layers in the slow cooker.
5. Cook on low for 8 to 10 hours. It shouldn't jiggle when it's done.
6. Cut into small rectangles and serve.

Lunch

Pulled Chicken Wraps

Prep Time: **10 minutes**; Cook Time: **6 hours**
Serving Size: **346g**; Serves: **2**; Calories: **270**
Total Fat: **7g** Saturated Fat: **1.8g**; Trans Fat: **0g**
Protein: **27.2g**; Net Carbs: **20.8g**
Total Carbs: **24.3g**; Dietary Fiber: **3.5g**; Sugars: **15.6g**
Cholesterol: 75mg; Sodium: 87mg; Potassium: 714mg; **Vitamin A**: 1%; **Vitamin C**: 47%; **Calcium**: 17%; **Iron**: 18%.

Ingredients:
- 2 chicken breasts
- 2 medium tomatoes, chopped
- 2 red onions, diced

- 2 garlic cloves, minced
- 1 tablespoon honey
- 1 teaspoon basil
- 1 teaspoon cloves, whole
- 3 tablespoons water

Directions:
1. Put the chicken into the slow cooker and add the chopped tomatoes, onions, garlic, honey, basil, cloves and water.
2. Cook on low for 6 hours. Shred the chicken with a fork and stir everything very well before serving.

Mediterranean Eggplant Salad

Prep Time: 10 minutes; Cook Time: 7-8 hours
Serving Size: **811g**; Serves: **2**; Calories: **194**
Total Fat: **0.7g** Saturated Fat: **0.2g**; Trans Fat: **0g**
Protein: **7.4g**; Net Carbs: **35.7g**
Total Carbs: **45.8g**; Dietary Fiber: **10.1g**; Sugars: **27.4g**
Cholesterol: 0mg; Sodium: 801mg; Potassium: 919mg; **Vitamin A**: 27%; **Vitamin C**: 380%; **Calcium**: 18%; **Iron**: 37%.

Ingredients:
- 1 red onion, sliced
- 2 bell peppers, sliced
- 1 large eggplant, quartered and sliced
- 1 (24-ounce) can whole tomatoes
- 2 teaspoons cumin

- 1 teaspoon salt
- juice of 1 lemon

Directions:
1. Place all the ingredients into a large slow cooker and cook on low for 7 to 8 hours.

Paleo Chicken Soup

Prep Time: 20 minutes; Cook Time: 8-10 hours
Serving Size: **1150g;** Serves: **4**; Calories: **318**
Total Fat: **1.9g** Saturated Fat: **0g;** Trans Fat: **0g**
Protein: **69.1g;** Net Carbs: **4.7g**
Total Carbs: **6.8g;** Dietary Fiber: **2.1g;** Sugars: **3.9g**
Cholesterol: 144mg; Sodium: 721mg; Potassium: 209mg;
Vitamin A: 105%; **Vitamin C**: 9%; **Calcium**: 5%; **Iron**: 1%.

Ingredients:
- 3 pounds chicken parts, skinless
- 12 cups water
- 4 stalks celery
- 2 carrots
- 1 ½ teaspoon minced garlic
- 1 cup pearl onions
- fresh baby spinach

Directions:

1. Pour 12 cups of water into the slow cooker. Add in all the remaining ingredients except for spinach and cook on low for 8 to 10 hours.
2. Remove the chicken, celery, carrots and onions from the pot and remove the meat from the bones.
3. Return everything back into the slow cooker and cook on high for 30 more minutes. Toss in the baby spinach and heat until it is wilted.

Cauliflower Bacon Soup

Prep Time: **5 minutes**; Cook Time: **5-6 hours**
Serving Size: **514g**; Serves: **4**; Calories: **330**
Total Fat: **1.7g** Saturated Fat: **0.7g**; Trans Fat: **0g**
Protein: **29.8g**; Net Carbs: **38.8g**
Total Carbs: **83.9g**; Dietary Fiber: **45.1g**; Sugars: **11.2g**
Cholesterol: **7mg**; Sodium: **767mg**; Potassium: **44mg**; Vitamin A: 17%; Vitamin C: 35%; Calcium: 15%; Iron: 20%.

Ingredients:
- 4 slices bacon
- 1 cup cauliflower florets
- 1 onion, chopped
- 3 cups water
- 1 package taco seasoning mix
- 2 (14-ounce) cans diced tomatoes, undrained

Directions:
1. Cook the bacon until crisp. Drain it on a paper towel and crumble.
2. In a slow cooker, combine the bacon, cauliflower, onion, water, seasoning and tomatoes.
3. Cook on low for 5 to 6 hours.

Egg Roll Soup

Prep Time: **10 minutes;** Cook Time: **5 hours**
Serving Size: **432g;** Serves: **6**; Calories: **255**
Total Fat: **13.2g** Saturated Fat: **5.5g**; Trans Fat: **0g**
Protein: **17.9g;** Net Carbs: **11.8g**
Total Carbs: **15.7g**; Dietary Fiber: **3.9g**; Sugars: **6.5g**
Cholesterol: 57mg; Sodium: 451mg; Potassium: 357mg;
Vitamin A: 180%; **Vitamin C**: 70%; **Calcium**: 7%; **Iron**: 7%.

Ingredients:
- 1 pound ground pastured pork
- 1 tablespoon ghee
- 1 large onion, diced
- 4 cups chicken stock
- ½ head cabbage, chopped
- 2 cups shredded carrots
- 1 teaspoon garlic powder
- 1 teaspoon onion powder
- 1 teaspoon sea salt

- 2/3 cup coconut aminos

Directions:
1. Heat the ghee in a skillet, toss in the pork and brown it for about 8 minutes.
2. Transfer the browned pork into the slow cooker and add all the remaining ingredients.
3. Cook on low for 5 hours.

Sausage Kale Soup

Prep Time: **10 minutes;** Cook Time: **6 hours**
Serving Size: **785g;** Serves: **4**; Calories: **498**
Total Fat: **32g** Saturated Fat: **10.3g;** Trans Fat: **0g**
Protein: **32.9g;** Net Carbs: **15.7g**
Total Carbs: **19.2g;** Dietary Fiber: **3.5g;** Sugars: **6.6g**
Cholesterol: 94mg; Sodium: 1947mg; Potassium: 951mg;
Vitamin A: 393%; **Vitamin C**: 147%; **Calcium**: 14%; **Iron**: 19%.

Ingredients:
- 3 cloves garlic, minced
- 1 large onion, chopped
- 2 cups chopped carrots
- 2 stalks celery, chopped
- 8 cups chicken stock
- 4 cups chopped kale
- 1 pound sausage

Directions:
1. Cook the sausage in a skillet and break it to pieces. Drain excess fat from the pan, retaining about 1 tablespoon.
2. In the reserved fat, sauté the garlic, onion, carrots and celery for about 4 to 5 minutes.
3. Place the sautéed vegetables into the slow cooker, pour in the chicken stock and add the sausage.
4. Cook for 6 hours on low. About 10 minutes before serving, add in the chopped kale and cook until wilted.

Butternut Squash Soup

Prep Time: 20 minutes; Cook Time: 6-8 hours
Serving Size: **618g;** Serves: **4**; Calories: **202**
Total Fat: **0.9g** Saturated Fat: **0g;** Trans Fat: **0g**
Protein: **5.5g;** Net Carbs: **35.5g**
Total Carbs: **49.1g;** Dietary Fiber: **13.6g;** Sugars: **17.1g**
Cholesterol: 0mg; Sodium: 326mg; Potassium: 1111mg;
Vitamin A: 118%; **Vitamin C**: 163%; **Calcium**: 14%; **Iron**: 91%.

Ingredients:
- 6 cups chopped butternut squash
- 2 medium apples, peeled, cored and chopped
- 2 medium carrots, peeled and chopped

- 1 small white onion, chopped
- 1 clove garlic, chopped
- 2 cups chicken stock
- 1 cup almond milk

Directions:
1. Place all the ingredients except for the almond milk into the slow cooker.
2. Cook on low for 6 to 8 hours.
3. Pour in the almond milk and stir well. Transfer everything to a food processor and process until perfectly smooth.
4. Serve warm.

Curry Pumpkin Soup

Prep Time: 5 minutes; Cook Time: 6-8 hours
Serving Size: **288g**; Serves: **4**; Calories: **142**
Total Fat: **4.9g** Saturated Fat: **4g**; Trans Fat: **0g**
Protein: **2.3g**; Net Carbs: **8g**
Total Carbs: **26.8g**; Dietary Fiber: **4.8g**; Sugars: **5g**
Cholesterol: **0mg**; Sodium: **9mg**; Potassium: **802mg**;
Vitamin A: 481%; **Vitamin C**: 79%; **Calcium**: 13%; **Iron**: 9%.

Ingredients:
- 2 pounds butternut pumpkin, raw
- 1 can coconut milk

- salt and pepper, to taste
- coconut oil, to taste

Directions:
1. Place the raw pumpkin, salt and pepper into the slow cooker and stir. Pour in the coconut milk - enough to cover the pumpkin completely. If necessary, add some water as well.
2. Cook on low for 6 to 8 hours. Add some coconut oil if you wish.

Vegetable Korma

Prep Time: **10 minutes;** Cook Time: **8 hours**
Serving Size: **360g;** Serves: **4;** Calories: **158**
Total Fat: **4.4g** Saturated Fat: **0.6g;** Trans Fat: **0g**
Protein: **8.2g;** Net Carbs: **16.1g**
Total Carbs: **26g;** Dietary Fiber: **9.9g;** Sugars: **10.4g**
Cholesterol: 0mg; Sodium: 480mg; Potassium: 914mg; **Vitamin A**: 129%; **Vitamin C**: 181%; **Calcium**: 11%; **Iron**: 11%.

Ingredients:
- 1 large cauliflower, cut into florets
- 2 large carrots, chopped
- 1 cup green beans, chopped
- ½ large onion, chopped
- 2 cloves garlic, minced
- ¾ can coconut milk
- 2 tablespoons curry powder
- 1 teaspoon sea salt
- 1 teaspoon garam marsala
- 2 tablespoons almond meal

Directions:
1. Place the chopped cauliflower, carrots, green beans, onion and garlic into the slow cooker. Stir well.
2. In a separate bowl, whisk together the coconut milk, curry powder, salt and garam masala. Pour this over the vegetables and sprinkle with almond meal.

3. Cook on low for 8 hours.
4. Serve warm or chilled.

Chicken Soup

Prep Time: **20 minutes**; Cook Time: **8 hours**
Serving Size: **645g**; Serves: **4**; Calories: **266**
Total Fat: **9g** Saturated Fat: **1.5g**; Trans Fat: **0g**
Protein: **31.3g**; Net Carbs: **13.6g**
Total Carbs: **18.1g**; Dietary Fiber: **4.5g**; Sugars: **11.5g**
Cholesterol: 65mg; Sodium: 1559mg; Potassium: 43mg;
Vitamin A: 18%; **Vitamin C**: 170%; **Calcium**: 5%; **Iron**: 9%.

Ingredients:
- 2 tablespoons olive oil
- 1 yellow onion, diced
- 1 red bell pepper, diced
- 1 jalapeño, diced
- 3 cloves garlic, minced
- 3-4 boneless, skinless chicken breasts
- 1 (28-ounce) can diced tomatoes
- 1 (4-ounce) can diced green chilies
- 4 cups chicken broth
- 1 teaspoon ground cumin

Directions:
1. Heat the olive oil in a skillet and sauté the diced onion, bell pepper, jalapeño and garlic until the onions turn translucent.

2. Transfer the vegetables into the slow cooker and add all the remaining ingredients.
3. Cook on low for 8 hours.
4. When done, remove the chicken and shred it with two forks to bite-size pieces. Return the chicken back into the slow cooker and stir everything well.
5. Ladle the soup into individual bowls and serve warm.

Dinner

Sweet Short Ribs with Ginger

Prep Time: 10 minutes; Cook Time: 6-8 hours
Serving Size: **180g;** Serves: **2**; Calories: **296**
Total Fat: **20.5g** Saturated Fat: **9g;** Trans Fat: **0g**
Protein: **9.2g;** Net Carbs: **16.5g**
Total Carbs: **18.6g;** Dietary Fiber: **2.1g;** Sugars: **15.7g**
Cholesterol: 42mg; Sodium: 28mg; Potassium: 188mg;
Vitamin A: 0%; **Vitamin C**: 30%; **Calcium**: 2%; **Iron**: 6%.

Ingredients:
- 1 beef short rib
- 2 small red onions, chopped
- 2 garlic cloves, minced
- 1 teaspoon ground ginger
- 1 tablespoon honey

Directions:
1. Pour about 1-inch depth of water into the slow cooker. Add all the ingredients.
2. Cover with the lid and cook on low for 6 to 8 hours.

Balsamic Blackberry Chicken

Prep Time: **5 minutes;** Cook Time: **4 hours**
Serving Size: **303g;** Serves: **2**; Calories: **220**
Total Fat: **3.8g** Saturated Fat: **1g;** Trans Fat: **0g**
Protein: **35.2g;** Net Carbs: **6.6g**
Total Carbs: **11.3g;** Dietary Fiber: **4.7g**; Sugars: **7.1g**
Cholesterol: **85mg;** Sodium: **290mg;** Potassium: **0mg;**
Vitamin A: 4%; **Vitamin C**: 29%; **Calcium**: 2%; **Iron**: 6%.

Ingredients:
- 2 chicken breasts, boneless and skinless
- 3 tablespoons balsamic vinegar
- ¼ teaspoon garlic powder
- 1 (6-ounce) package fresh blackberries

Directions:
1. Place all the ingredients into the slow cooker.
2. Cook for 4 hours on low.

Slow-Cooked Beef with Root Veggies and Kale

Prep Time: **15 minutes**; Cook Time: **6 hours**
Serving Size: **260g**; Serves: **4**; Calories: **298**
Total Fat: **9.2g** Saturated Fat: **3.2g**; Trans Fat: **0g**
Protein: **35.8g**; Net Carbs: **12.7g**
Total Carbs: **15.8g**; Dietary Fiber: **3.1g**; Sugars: **5.4g**
Cholesterol: 98mg; Sodium: 99mg; Potassium: 692mg;
Vitamin A: 205%; **Vitamin C**: 89%; **Calcium**: 8%; **Iron**: 19%.

Ingredients:
- 14 ounces beef braising steak, cut into chunks
- 2 red onions, chopped
- 2 large carrots, chopped
- ½ celeriac, skin removed and chopped into cubes
- ½ swede, skin removed and chopped into cubes
- 6 garlic cloves, minced
- water
- 2 cups kale, fresh

Directions:
1. Pour about 2 inches of water into the slow cooker and add in all the ingredients, except for the kale.
2. Cover and cook on low for 6 hours. When done, toss in the kale, place the lid back on and let it cook for another 5 to 10 minutes.

Slow Cooker Chicken Chili

Prep Time: **5 minutes**; Cook Time: **6-8 hours**
Serving Size: **619g**; Serves: **4**; Calories: **554**
Total Fat: **30.2g** Saturated Fat: **9g**; Trans Fat: **0g**
Protein: **60.4g**; Net Carbs: **12.7g**
Total Carbs: **17.4g**; Dietary Fiber: **4.7g**; Sugars: **9.9g**
Cholesterol: 270mg; Sodium: 1148mg; Potassium: 1173mg;
Vitamin A: 21%; **Vitamin C**: 103%; **Calcium**: 10%; **Iron**: 14%.

Ingredients:
- 8-12 chicken thighs, boneless and skinless
- 1 (16-ounce) jar salsa
- 1 (16-ounce) can diced tomatoes
- 1 medium yellow onion, chopped
- 1 large red pepper, chopped
- 2 tablespoons chili powder

Directions:
1. Roughly chop the chicken thighs into 1-inch pieces and place them into the slow cooker.
2. Add in all the remaining ingredients and stir.
3. Cover with a lid and cook on low for 6 to 8 hours.

Perfect Slow Cooker Roast Chicken

Prep Time: **10 minutes**; Cook Time: **4 hours**

Serving Size: **317g**; Serves: **4**; Calories: **463**

Total Fat: **28.2g** Saturated Fat: **8g**; Trans Fat: **0g**

Protein: **41.4g;** Net Carbs: **8g**

Total Carbs: **10.3g**; Dietary Fiber: **2.1g**; Sugars: **4.2g**

Cholesterol: 191mg; Sodium: 595mg; Potassium: 154mg;

Vitamin A: 106%; **Vitamin C**: 26%; **Calcium**: 8%; **Iron**: 15%.

Ingredients:
- 1 (4-pound) whole chicken
- 1 yellow onion, quartered
- 1 head garlic, halved
- 1 lemon, quartered
- 1 tablespoon paprika
- 1 teaspoon sea salt
- 1 teaspoon dried thyme
- 2 carrots

Directions:
1. Mix the paprika, salt and thyme in a small bowl and rub the chicken, including its cavity, with this mix.
2. Stuff the chicken's cavity with half of the garlic, two quarters of the onion and two quarters of lemon. Alternate once more.
3. Tie the legs together, so the stuffing stays in place.

4. Place the carrots into the slow cooker, then place the chicken on top of it. Rub the chicken generously with some more paprika to give it a crispier look when done.
5. Cover and cook on high for 4 hours.

Simple Beef Stew

Prep Time: **10 minutes**; Cook Time: **8 hours**
Serving Size: **441g**; Serves: **5**; Calories: **450**
Total Fat: **11.3g** Saturated Fat: **4.3g**; Trans Fat: **0g**
Protein: **58.4g**; Net Carbs: **22.2g**
Total Carbs: **25.3g**; Dietary Fiber: **3.1g**; Sugars: **4.1g**
Cholesterol: 161mg; Sodium: 357mg; Potassium: 1209mg;
Vitamin A: 83%; **Vitamin C**: 18%; **Calcium**: 3%; **Iron**: 191%.

Ingredients:
- 2 pounds pastured stewing beef
- 2 cups chicken stock
- 1 tablespoon balsamic vinegar
- 1 medium onion, chopped
- 2 stalks celery, roughly chopped
- 2 large carrots, peeled and chopped
- 4 small sweet potatoes, cubed
- 1 clove garlic, minced
- 3 bay leaves
- salt, to taste
- 1 teaspoon dried basil
- 1 teaspoon dried rosemary

Directions:

1. Place the meat into the slow cooker. Pour in the chicken stock and balsamic vinegar. Add all the remaining ingredients.
2. Cover and let it cook for 8 hours on low.

Lamb Stew

Prep Time: 10 minutes; Cook Time: 7-8 hours
Serving Size: **465g**; Serves: **4**; Calories: **715**
Total Fat: **32.7g** Saturated Fat: **14.9g**; Trans Fat: **0g**
Protein: **64.2g**; Net Carbs: **33.7g**
Total Carbs: **40.2g**; Dietary Fiber: **6.5g**; Sugars: **25.4g**
Cholesterol: 224mg; Sodium: 192mg; Potassium: 1456mg;
Vitamin A: 36%; **Vitamin C**: 117%; **Calcium**: 6%; **Iron**: 56%.

Ingredients:
- 2 pounds lamb, diced
- 2 sweet potatoes, peeled and diced
- 1 red bell pepper, diced
- 1 cup dried apricots, diced
- 1 can crushed tomatoes
- 3 tablespoons ghee

Directions:
1. Heat the ghee in a skillet and toss in the diced lamb. Quickly sear the meat.
2. Transfer the lamb, with the rest of the ingredients, into the slow cooker and cook on low for 7 to 8 hours.

Chicken Curry

Prep Time: **15 minutes**; Cook Time: **10 hours**
Serving Size: **395g**; Serves: **6**; Calories: **429**
Total Fat: **22g** Saturated Fat: **16g**; Trans Fat: **0g**
Protein: **49.7g**; Net Carbs: **9.8g**
Total Carbs: **13.9g**; Dietary Fiber: **4.1g**; Sugars: **6.5g**
Cholesterol: 131mg; Sodium: 1149mg; Potassium: 942mg;
Vitamin A: 175%; **Vitamin C**: 15%; **Calcium**: 4%; **Iron**: 19%.

Ingredients:
- 3 pounds boneless chicken breasts
- 1 onion, chopped
- 6 cloves garlic, minced
- 1 ½ teaspoons fish sauce
- 2 ½ teaspoons salt
- 2 ½ teaspoons ground cumin
- 1 ½ teaspoons ground turmeric
- 1 ½ teaspoons ground coriander
- ¾ teaspoon ground nutmeg
- 1 (15-ounce) can coconut milk
- 5 large carrots, chopped
- 3 cups broccoli florets
- 1 container mushrooms

Directions:
1. Put the chicken, onion, garlic, fish sauce, salt, cumin, turmeric, coriander and nutmeg into the slow cooker and cook on low for 5 hours.

2. After about 5 hours, add the coconut milk, carrots, broccoli and mushrooms. Remove the chicken and shred it to bite-size pieces, then return the pieces back into the slow cooker and cook everything for about 5 hours more.
3. Serve right away.

Carnitas Lettuce Wraps with Pineapple and Salsa

Prep Time: 15 minutes; Cook Time: 8-10 hours
Serving Size: **275g**; Serves: **6**; Calories: **424**
Total Fat: **30.7g** Saturated Fat: **8.9g**; Trans Fat: **0g**
Protein: **28g**; Net Carbs: **8g**
Total Carbs: **11.6g**; Dietary Fiber: **3.6g**; Sugars: **5.8g**
Cholesterol: 106mg; Sodium: 232mg; Potassium: 292mg;
Vitamin A: 27%; **Vitamin C**: 71%; **Calcium**: 2%; **Iron**: 12%.

Ingredients:
For the carnitas
- ¼ teaspoon dried oregano
- ½ teaspoon ground cumin
- ½ teaspoon garlic powder
- ½ teaspoon sea salt
- 1 tablespoon olive oil
- 2 pounds bone-in pork shoulder
- 1 onion, chopped

- 1 orange, juiced
- 2 tablespoons squeezed lemon juice

For the pineapple and avocado salsa
- ¾ cup diced fresh pineapple
- ½ cup diced red onion
- ¼ cup chopped fresh cilantro
- 1 tablespoon squeezed lemon juice
- salt, to taste
- 1 avocado, peeled and cubed
- 1 head lettuce, separated into leaves, for serving

Directions:
1. In a small bowl, mix together the oregano, cumin, garlic powder, salt and olive oil. Pat the pork dry with a paper towel and rub it with the mixed spices.
2. Place the meat into the slow cooker and add the onion, orange and lemon juice. Cook for 8 to 10 hours on low.
3. Preheat the broiler, then remove the pork from the slow cooker and shred it to bite-size pieces. Place the shredded pork onto a baking sheet, drizzle with ¼ of the cooking liquid and broil for about 3 to 5 minutes.
4. For the salsa, stir together all the ingredients except for the avocado cubes. Finally toss in the avocado as well and gently stir.
5. Serve the salsa over the pork inside the lettuce leaves.

Chicken Ropa Vieja

Prep Time: **15 minutes;** Cook Time: **4 hours**
Serving Size: **428g;** Serves: **4**; Calories: **255**
Total Fat: **1.3g** Saturated Fat: **0g;** Trans Fat: **0g**
Protein: **47.9g;** Net Carbs: **10.8g**
Total Carbs: **14.9g;** Dietary Fiber: **4.1g;** Sugars: **8.5g**
Cholesterol: 96mg; Sodium: 667mg; Potassium: 214mg;
Vitamin A: 14%; **Vitamin C**: 141%; **Calcium**: 4%; **Iron**: 9%.

Ingredients:
- 2 pounds chicken pieces, boneless and skinless
- 4 cloves garlic, minced
- ½ tablespoon oregano
- 1 medium yellow onion, sliced
- 1 medium green bell pepper, chopped
- 1 medium red bell pepper, chopped
- 1 (15-ounce) can diced tomatoes
- 3 tablespoons tomato paste
- salt, to taste

Directions:
1. Place the chicken into the slow cooker, add the minced garlic, oregano, onion, bell peppers, diced tomatoes and tomato paste. Season with salt.
2. Cover with the lid and cook on high for 4 hours.

3. When done, shred the chicken and stir everything well. Cook without the lid for 15 additional minutes.
4. Serve warm.

Country Cooking Slow Cooker Neck Bones

Prep Time: **15 minutes;** Cook Time: **4 hours**
Serving Size: **245g**; Serves: **6**; Calories: **706**
Total Fat: **59.7g** Saturated Fat: **21.8g**; Trans Fat: **0g**
Protein: **38.1g**; Net Carbs: **3.8g**
Total Carbs: **4.2g**; Dietary Fiber: **0.4g**; Sugars: **2.8g**
Cholesterol: 179mg; Sodium: 3386mg; Potassium: 33mg;
Vitamin A: 0%; **Vitamin C**: 3%; **Calcium**: 1%; **Iron**: 24%.

Ingredients:
- 3 pounds pork neck bones
- 1 small onion, chopped
- 3 cloves garlic, minced
- 1 tablespoon white vinegar
- 4 cups water

Directions:
1. Place the pork neck bones into the slow cooker. Add the chopped onion, garlic, vinegar and water.
2. Cover and cook on high for about 4 hours.

Lemon Chicken

Prep Time: 15 minutes; Cook Time: 8-10 hours
Serving Size: **195g**; Serves: **4**; Calories: **325**

Total Fat: **20g** Saturated Fat: **2g**; Trans Fat: **0g**
Protein: **32.2g**; Net Carbs: **1.2g**
Total Carbs: **1.3g**; Dietary Fiber: **0.1g**; Sugars: **0.3g**
Cholesterol: 140mg; Sodium: 144mg; Potassium: 28mg;
Vitamin A: 3%; **Vitamin C**: 18%; **Calcium**: 1%; **Iron**: 9%.

Ingredients:
- 2 cloves garlic, minced
- 4 tablespoons olive oil
- 2 tablespoons chopped parsley
- 3 tablespoons lemon juice
- 8 chicken thighs

Directions:
1. Place the minced garlic, olive oil, parsley, lemon juice and chicken in a zip-top freezer bag and coat the chicken.
2. Transfer all the ingredients into the slow cooker, cover and cook on low for 8 to 10 hours.

Honey-Dijon Chicken

Prep Time: 10 minutes; Cook Time: 8-10 hours
Serving Size: **150g**; Serves: **8**; Calories: **271**
Total Fat: **15.6g** Saturated Fat: **2.5g**; Trans Fat: **0g**
Protein: **24g**; Net Carbs: **8g**
Total Carbs: **10g**; Dietary Fiber: **0g**; Sugars: **10g**
Cholesterol: **60mg**; Sodium: **353mg**; Potassium: **6mg**;
Vitamin A: 0%; **Vitamin C**: 0%; **Calcium**: 0%; **Iron**: 0%.

Ingredients:
- 2 pounds chicken breasts, boneless and skinless
- 1 ½ teaspoons garlic powder
- 1 teaspoon onion powder
- 2 cups honey-Dijon mustard (no added sugar)

Directions:
1. Grease the slow cooker with nonstick cooking spray and put the chicken breasts in. Season with onion and garlic powder and pour in the honey-Dijon mustard.
2. Cover and cook on low for 8 to 10 hours.

Slow Cooker Bacon and Chicken

Prep Time: **10 minutes;** Cook Time: **8 hours**
Serving Size: **176g;** Serves: **4;** Calories: **373**
Total Fat: **27.9g** Saturated Fat: **4.7g;** Trans Fat: **0g**
Protein: **33.4g;** Net Carbs: **0.2g**
Total Carbs: **0.2g;** Dietary Fiber: **0g;** Sugars: **0g**
Cholesterol: 86mg; Sodium: 653mg; Potassium: 352mg;
Vitamin A: 0%; **Vitamin C**: 0%; **Calcium**: 0%; **Iron**: 6%.

Ingredients:
- 5 chicken breasts
- 10 slices bacon
- 2 tablespoons dried thyme
- 1 tablespoon dried oregano
- 5 tablespoons olive oil
- salt, to taste

Directions:
1. Put all the ingredients into the slow cooker and stir.
2. Cook on low for 8 hours.
3. Before serving shred the meat and sprinkle with some olive oil.

Butter Chicken

Prep Time: **10 minutes**; Cook Time: **5 hours**
Serving Size: **502g**; Serves: **4**; Calories: **487**
Total Fat: **15.5g** Saturated Fat: **9g**; Trans Fat: **0g**
Protein: **68.2g**; Net Carbs: **14.7g**
Total Carbs: **18.2g**; Dietary Fiber: **3.5g**; Sugars: **9.8g**
Cholesterol: 181mg; Sodium: 1145mg; Potassium: 580mg;
Vitamin A: 23%; **Vitamin C**: 22%; **Calcium**: 11%; **Iron**: 9%.

Ingredients:
- 1 tablespoon coconut oil
- 3 cloves garlic, crushed
- 1 onion, diced
- 1 ¾ cup coconut milk
- ¾ cup tomato paste
- 2 tablespoons arrowroot flour
- 2 teaspoons garam masala
- ½ teaspoon ground ginger
- sea salt, to taste
- 2 1/5 pounds chicken breast, skinless

Directions:
1. Heat the coconut oil in a skillet, add the garlic and diced onion and sauté for about 3 minutes, stirring frequently.
2. Add in the coconut milk, tomato paste, arrowroot flour, garam masala, ginger and salt.

3. Place the chicken breasts into the slow cooker and add the sauce from the skillet. Cover and let it cook on low for 5 hours.

Ratatouille

Prep Time: 10 minutes; Cook Time: 5-6 hours
Serving Size: **465g**; Serves: **4**; Calories: **171**
Total Fat: **7.7g** Saturated Fat: **6.1g**; Trans Fat: **0g**
Protein: **5.6g**; Net Carbs: **15.5g**
Total Carbs: **25g**; Dietary Fiber: **9.5g**; Sugars: **11.4g**
Cholesterol: 0mg; Sodium: 422mg; Potassium: 1141mg;
Vitamin A: 21%; **Vitamin C**: 158%; **Calcium**: 7%; **Iron**: 16%.

Ingredients:
- 2 tablespoons coconut oil
- 1 large onion, chopped
- 6 cloves garlic, minced
- 1 large eggplant, chopped
- 1 orange bell pepper, chopped
- 4 zucchini
- 1 cup chopped grape tomatoes
- 2 tablespoons tomato paste
- 1 teaspoon dried oregano
- 1 teaspoon sea salt
- 1 cup fresh basil, chopped

Directions:
1. Place all the ingredients except for the fresh basil into a slow cooker. Cover and cook for 5 to 6 hours on low.
2. Before serving, stir in the fresh basil.

Roasted Chicken

Prep Time: **5 minutes;** Cook Time: **5-6 hours**
Serving Size: **368g**; Serves: **6**; Calories: **396**
Total Fat: **10.8g** Saturated Fat: **4g**; Trans Fat: **0g**
Protein: **67.5g;** Net Carbs: **3.4g**
Total Carbs: **4.8g;** Dietary Fiber: **1.4g**; Sugars: **2.4g**
Cholesterol: 174mg; Sodium: 417mg; Potassium: 199mg;
Vitamin A: 138%; **Vitamin C**: 5%; **Calcium**: 2%; **Iron**: 12%.

Ingredients:
- 3-4 pounds roasted chicken
- 3-4 stalks celery, cut into 2-inch pieces
- 4-5 whole carrots, cut into 2-inch pieces
- 1 teaspoon salt
- 1 teaspoon pepper
- 1 teaspoon paprika

Directions:
1. Place all the ingredients into the slow cooker. Cover and cook on low for 5 to 6 hours.

Sausage and Peppers

Prep Time: **20 minutes;** Cook Time: **6 hours**
Serving Size: **171g;** Serves: **8;** Calories: **228**
Total Fat: **15.4g** Saturated Fat: **5.4g;** Trans Fat: **0g**
Protein: **12g;** Net Carbs: **8.6g**
Total Carbs: **10.9g;** Dietary Fiber: **2.3g;** Sugars: **4.4g**
Cholesterol: 32mg; Sodium: 788mg; Potassium: 322mg;
Vitamin A: 6%; **Vitamin C**: 122%; **Calcium**: 3%; **Iron**: 15%.

Ingredients:
- 1 pound mild chicken Italian sausage, cooked and chopped
- 1 green pepper, chopped
- 1 red pepper, chopped
- 1 yellow pepper, chopped
- 1 medium onion, chopped
- 6 cloves garlic, minced
- 1 teaspoon dried oregano
- ¼ cup fresh basil, chopped
- 1 (14-ounce) can diced tomatoes
- 2 tablespoons tomato paste

Directions:
1. Put the sausage, peppers, onion, garlic, dried oregano and basil into the slow cooker.

2. Stir in the diced tomatoes and paste. Cook on low for 6 hours.
3. Right before it is done, cut the sausage into bite-size pieces and stir well.
4. Serve warm.

Pork with Kale

Prep Time: 10 minutes; Cook Time: 8-10 hours
Serving Size: **297g**; Serves: **8**; Calories: **339**
Total Fat: **13.2g** Saturated Fat: **4.8g**; Trans Fat: **0g**
Protein: **42g**; Net Carbs: **8.8g**
Total Carbs: **11.4g**; Dietary Fiber: **2.6g**; Sugars: **3.6g**
Cholesterol: 111mg; Sodium: 316mg; Potassium: 872mg;
Vitamin A: 189%; **Vitamin C**: 131%; **Calcium**: 12%; **Iron**: 16%.

Ingredients:
- 2 ½ pounds pork loin chops
- 7 cups chopped kale
- 1 (28-ounce) can diced tomatoes
- 2 tablespoons garlic powder
- 1 tablespoon onion powder
- 1 tablespoon balsamic vinegar

Directions:
1. Layer all the ingredients into the slow cooker. Pork chops should be at the bottom and diced tomatoes on top.
2. Cook on low for 8 to 10 hours.

Balsamic Beef

Prep Time: 10 minutes; Cook Time: 6-8 hours
Serving Size: **196g**; Serves: **8**; Calories: **253**
Total Fat: **8.8g** Saturated Fat: **2.9g**; Trans Fat: **0g**
Protein: **34.8g**; Net Carbs: **5.2g**
Total Carbs: **6.4g**; Dietary Fiber: **1.2g**; Sugars: **4.3g**
Cholesterol: 100mg; Sodium: 184mg; Potassium: 479mg;
Vitamin A: 4%; **Vitamin C**: 9%; **Calcium**: 2%; **Iron**: 121%.

Ingredients:
- 1 tablespoon olive oil
- 2 pounds ground steak, cut into 1 inch pieces
- 1 teaspoon dried oregano
- 1 teaspoon dried basil
- 1 medium onion, thinly sliced
- 4 cloves garlic, minced
- ½ cup balsamic vinegar
- 2 (14.5-ounce) cans diced tomatoes

Directions:
1. Grease the slow cooker with olive oil. Add in the beef and season it with oregano and basil. Add the onion, garlic, vinegar and tomatoes.
2. Cook on low for 6 to 8 hours.

Slow Cooked Turkey Breasts

Prep Time: 20 minutes; Cook Time: 3-4 hours
Serving Size: **375g**; Serves: **6**; Calories: **402**
Total Fat: **6.7g** Saturated Fat: **0g**; Trans Fat: **0g**
Protein: **87g**; Net Carbs: **8g**
Total Carbs: **0g**; Dietary Fiber: **0g**; Sugars: **0g**
Cholesterol: 134mg; Sodium: 2344mg; Potassium: 0mg;
Vitamin A: 0%; **Vitamin C**: 0%; **Calcium**: 0%; **Iron**: 13%.

Ingredients:
- 5 pounds turkey breast
- 1 ½ cups water
- ½ teaspoon rosemary
- ½ teaspoon thyme

Directions:
1. Place all the ingredients into the slow cooker and cook on high for about 1 hour. Then reduce to low and cook for another 2 to 3 hours.

Spicy Chicken Taco Meat

Prep Time: **5 minutes**; Cook Time: **8 hours**
Serving Size: **302g**; Serves: **6**; Calories: **150**
Total Fat: **2.7g** Saturated Fat: **0.7g**; Trans Fat: **0g**

Protein: **24.1g;** Net Carbs: **8g**
Total Carbs: **8.4g;** Dietary Fiber: **2.1g;** Sugars: **4.2g**
Cholesterol: 57mg; Sodium: 407mg; Potassium: 310mg;
Vitamin A: 6%; **Vitamin C**: 48%; **Calcium**: 5%; **Iron**: 8%.

Ingredients:
- 4-5 chicken breasts, frozen
- ½ onion, diced
- 1 green bell pepper, diced
- 4 garlic gloves, minced
- 1 (28-ounce) can whole tomatoes, crushed with fork
- 2-4 chipotle peppers in adobe sauce, chopped

Directions:
1. Place the chicken into the slow cooker and add all the remaining ingredients.
2. Cook on low for 8 hours. When done shred the chicken and serve right away.

Rotisserie Chicken

Prep Time: **5 minutes;** Cook Time: **8 hours**
Serving Size: **300g;** Serves: **6**; Calories: **563**
Total Fat: **37.5g** Saturated Fat: **13.4g;** Trans Fat: **0g**
Protein: **56.3g;** Net Carbs: **8g**
Total Carbs: **0g;** Dietary Fiber: **0g;** Sugars: **0g**
Cholesterol: 214mg; Sodium: 474mg; Potassium: 0mg;
Vitamin A: 0%; **Vitamin C:** 0%; **Calcium:** 0%; **Iron:** 16%.

Ingredients:
- 1 broiler/fryer chicken (3.5-4 pounds)
- 2 tablespoons paprika
- 1 ½ teaspoon onion powder
- 3 cloves garlic, minced
- 1 teaspoon salt

Directions:
1. Stir the paprika, onion powder, garlic and salt in a small bowl and add a few teaspoons of water, until a paste forms. Rub the chicken with this paste.
2. Grease the slow cooker with cooking spray and place the chicken in, breast-side up.
3. Cook on low for 8 hours.

Whole Chicken in the Slow Cooker

Prep Time: **10 minutes**; Cook Time: **7 hours**
Serving Size: **390g**; Serves: **5**; Calories: **687**
Total Fat: **45g** Saturated Fat: **12.9g**; Trans Fat: **0g**
Protein: **64.6g**; Net Carbs: **8g**
Total Carbs: **2.8g**; Dietary Fiber: **0.6g**; Sugars: **1.3g**
Cholesterol: 305mg; Sodium: 602mg; Potassium: 44mg;
Vitamin A: 6%; **Vitamin C**: 4%; **Calcium**: 7%; **Iron**: 19%.

Ingredients:
- 2 teaspoons paprika
- 1 teaspoon salt
- 1 teaspoon onion powder
- 1 teaspoon dried thyme
- ½ teaspoon garlic powder
- 1 large onion, peeled and cut into wedges
- 1 large whole chicken (about 4 pounds)

Directions:
1. Mix all the spices in a small bowl.
2. Layer the onion on the bottom of the slow cooker.
3. Rub the spices all over the chicken. Then place the chicken breast-side-down onto the onion in the slow cooker.
4. Cover and cook on low for 7 hours.
5. When done, remove the meat from the bones and serve.

Slow Cooked Chicken Thighs

Prep Time: 10 minutes; Cook Time: 3 ½ hours
Serving Size: **353g**; Serves: **4**; Calories: **309**
Total Fat: **14.3g** Saturated Fat: **2g**; Trans Fat: **0g**
Protein: **32.5g**; Net Carbs: **7.9g**
Total Carbs: **9.8g;** Dietary Fiber: **1.9g**; Sugars: **3.8g**
Cholesterol: 137mg; Sodium: 146mg; Potassium: 271mg;
Vitamin A: 8%; **Vitamin C**: 43%; **Calcium**: 7%; **Iron**: 23%.

Ingredients:
- 1 ½ pounds chicken thighs
- 2 tablespoons olive oil
- 3 cloves garlic, minced
- ½ teaspoon turmeric powder
- 1 red onion, chopped
- 3 tomatoes, chopped
- 1 teaspoon cayenne pepper
- ½ teaspoon cumin powder
- ½ teaspoon coriander powder
- 1 can coconut milk
- ¼ cup chopped cilantro

Directions:
1. Put all the ingredients except for the coconut milk and cilantro into the slow cooker. Stir and cook for 2 ½ hours on high.
2. Pour in the coconut milk and cook for 1 more hour.

3. Before serving, sprinkle with fresh cilantro.

Slow Cooker Brisket with Onions

Prep Time: **5 minutes**; Cook Time: **6 hours**
Serving Size: **375g**; Serves: **4**; Calories: **713**
Total Fat: **45.3g** Saturated Fat: **21.3g**; Trans Fat: **0g**
Protein: **62.6g**; Net Carbs: **6.2g**
Total Carbs: **11g**; Dietary Fiber: **4.8g**; Sugars: **9.7g**
Cholesterol: 188mg; Sodium: 3221mg; Potassium: 116mg;
Vitamin A: 12%; **Vitamin C**: 8%; **Calcium**: 9%; **Iron**: 31%.

Ingredients:
- 1 large red onion, thinly sliced
- 3 garlic cloves, minced
- 1 first cut of beef brisket (2 pounds), trimmed of excess fat
- 2 cups beef broth

Directions:
1. Place the sliced onion and minced garlic into the slow cooker. Add the beef brisket and broth.
2. Cover and cook for 6 hours on high.
3. Remove the meat onto a cutting board and thinly slice it.
4. Strain the onions from the broth and arrange them on a platter.
5. Transfer the broth into a skillet and let it boil for 5 minutes, then transfer it into a gravy boat.

6. Place the sliced meat on top of the onions and serve with the gravy on the side.

Thai Chicken Breasts

Prep Time: 10 minutes; Cook Time: 4-6 hours
Serving Size: **378g**; Serves: **4**; Calories: **480**
Total Fat: **29.9g** Saturated Fat: **23.7g**; Trans Fat: **0g**
Protein: **38.2g**; Net Carbs: **9.3g**
Total Carbs: **13.4g**; Dietary Fiber: **4.1g**; Sugars: **7.1g**
Cholesterol: 85mg; Sodium: 457mg; Potassium: 382mg;
Vitamin A: 121%; **Vitamin C**: 28%; **Calcium**: 5%; **Iron**: 12%.

Ingredients:
- 4 chicken breasts
- ¼ teaspoon ground turmeric
- ¼ teaspoon cumin
- 15 ounces light coconut milk
- ¼ cup fresh cilantro
- 2 carrots, chopped

Directions:
1. Season the chicken and place it into the slow cooker. Add the coconut milk, cilantro and carrots.
2. Cook on low for 4 to 6 hours.

Leg of Lamb with Parsnips

Prep Time: **15 minutes**; Cook Time: **8 hours**
Serving Size: **265g**; Serves: **4**; Calories: **200**

Total Fat: **7g** Saturated Fat: **1.9g;** Trans Fat: **0g**
Protein: **7.6g;** Net Carbs: **22.6g**
Total Carbs: **28.9g;** Dietary Fiber: **6.3g;** Sugars: **9.6g**
Cholesterol: 0mg; Sodium: 533mg; Potassium: 664mg;
Vitamin A: 153%; **Vitamin C**: 36%; **Calcium**: 7%; **Iron**: 6%.

Ingredients:
- 1 tablespoon olive oil
- 1 3-pound boneless leg of lamb, tied or with oven safe netting
- 1 teaspoon salt
- ½ teaspoon black pepper
- 1 large onion, diced
- 3 carrots, peeled and diced
- 3 parsnips, peeled and diced
- 2 cloves garlic, minced
- ½ cup beef broth

Directions:
1. Heat the olive oil in a skillet and brown the lamb on all sides.
2. Place the onion, carrots, parsnips and garlic into the slow cooker. Season with salt and pepper.
3. Add in the browned lamb, pour in the broth and cook on low for 8 hours.
4. When done, serve the lamb with the vegetables.

Slow Cooker Italian Chicken

Prep Time: **30 minutes**; Cook Time: **7 hours**
Serving Size: **438g**; Serves: **6**; Calories: **407**
Total Fat: **9g** Saturated Fat: **0.7g**; Trans Fat: **0g**
Protein: **70.4g**; Net Carbs: **9.4g**
Total Carbs: **11.4g**; Dietary Fiber: **2g**; Sugars: **4.3g**
Cholesterol: 173mg; Sodium: 213mg; Potassium: 322mg;
Vitamin A: 1%; **Vitamin C**: 39%; **Calcium**: 6%; **Iron**: 27%.

Ingredients:
- 4 pounds chicken breasts, boneless and skinless
- 5 medium tomatoes, chopped
- 1 onion, chopped
- 3 tablespoons garlic, minced
- 2 tablespoons tomato paste
- 2 tablespoons olive oil
- 1 tablespoon honey
- 2 tablespoons Italian seasoning
- sea salt and pepper, to taste

Directions:
1. Toss all the ingredients except for the chicken together in a medium bowl.
2. Place the chicken and the remaining ingredients into the slow cooker and cook on low for 7 hours.

3. When done, remove the chicken and shred it to bite-size pieces. Return the pieces back into the slow cooker and cook for 30 more minutes.

Fiesta Chicken

Prep Time: **5 minutes;** Cook Time: **8 hours**
Serving Size: **398g;** Serves: **6**; Calories: **325**
Total Fat: **8.1g** Saturated Fat: **3g;** Trans Fat: **0g**
Protein: **52g;** Net Carbs: **7.4g**
Total Carbs: **10.4g;** Dietary Fiber: **3g;** Sugars: **5.9g**
Cholesterol: 131mg; Sodium: 403mg; Potassium: 39mg;
Vitamin A: 13%; **Vitamin C**: 23%; **Calcium**: 4%; **Iron**: 11%.

Ingredients:
- 3 pounds chicken breasts
- 32 ounces whole or diced tomatoes
- 1 onion, sliced
- 6 cloves garlic, minced
- 3 tablespoons cumin
- salt and pepper, to taste

Directions:
1. Put all the ingredients into the slow cooker.
2. Cook on low for 8 hours.
3. After about 4 hours, shred the chicken with forks and cook for the remaining 4 hours.

Slow Cooker Ham

Prep Time: **5 minutes**; Cook Time: **4-6 hours**
Serving Size: **258g**; Serves: **8**; Calories: **383**
Total Fat: **19.6g** Saturated Fat: **10.1g**; Trans Fat: **0g**
Protein: **43.1g**; Net Carbs: **10.9g**
Total Carbs: **11g**; Dietary Fiber: **0.1g**; Sugars: **10.7g**
Cholesterol: 116mg; Sodium: 622mg; Potassium: 775mg;
Vitamin A: 0%; **Vitamin C**: 24%; **Calcium**: 1%; **Iron**: 12%.

Ingredients:
- 1 (4-6 pound) ham roast
- ¼ cup honey
- ½ cup fresh lemon juice
- 2 teaspoons dried rosemary
- 4 tablespoons coconut oil
- zest of 1 orange
- 1 teaspoon apple cider vinegar

Directions:
1. Put the ham roast into the slow cooker, then add the remaining ingredients.
2. Cook on low for 4 to 6 hours.

Slow Cooker Meatballs

Prep Time: **5 minutes**; Cook Time: **5-6 hours**

Serving Size: **170g;** Serves: **8**; Calories: **332**
Total Fat: **17.9g** Saturated Fat: **7.9g;** Trans Fat: **0g**
Protein: **16.6g;** Net Carbs: **8g**
Total Carbs: **28.6g;** Dietary Fiber: **2.1g;** Sugars: **17.8g**
Cholesterol: 64mg; Sodium: 854mg; Potassium: 248mg;
Vitamin A: 6%; **Vitamin C**: 4%; **Calcium**: 4%; **Iron**: 22%.

Ingredients:
- 1 (28-ounce) package frozen, bite-sized, fully-cooked Italian meatballs
- 1 (8-ounce) can crushed pineapple

Directions:
1. Put all the ingredients into the slow cooker, stir and cook on low for 5 to 6 hours.

Braised Short Ribs

Prep Time: 20 minutes; Cook Time: 8-10 hours
Serving Size: **356g;** Serves: **8**; Calories: **932**
Total Fat: **83.6g** Saturated Fat: **36.2g;** Trans Fat: **0g**
Protein: **33.1g;** Net Carbs: **6.3g**
Total Carbs: **9.2g;** Dietary Fiber: **2.9g;** Sugars: **5.1g**
Cholesterol: 169mg; Sodium: 264mg; Potassium: 172mg;
Vitamin A: 160%; **Vitamin C**: 11%; **Calcium**: 7%; **Iron**: 24%.

Ingredients:
- 1 tablespoon olive oil
- 4 pounds (about 8 ribs) beef short ribs
- 1 medium onion, chopped
- 3 cloves garlic, minced
- ½ cup sliced fresh mushrooms
- 2 beef stock cubes
- ½ cup water
- 1 (14.5-ounce) can diced tomatoes, undrained
- 1 pound peeled baby carrots
- 1 small bay leaf
- ½ teaspoon dried thyme
- 1 teaspoon olive oil
- salt and pepper, to taste

Directions:
1. Heat the olive oil in a skillet and brown the beef short ribs. Transfer them to a slow cooker.
2. Toss the onion, garlic and mushrooms into the skillet and sauté for about 3 to 5 minutes.
3. Deglaze the skillet with water. Add the beef stock cubes, tomatoes, baby carrots, bay leaf and thyme. Stir well.
4. Pour the mixture from the skillet into the slow cooker, cover and cook on low for 8 to 10 hours.
5. Transfer the cooked ribs onto a serving platter and the cooking juices into a skillet.
6. Cook for about 5 minutes in the skillet to get a proper sauce.
7. Pour the sauce over the ribs when serving.

Shredded Beef Tacos

Prep Time: **40 minutes**; Cook Time: **8 hours**
Serving Size: **399g**; Serves: **4**; Calories: **545**
Total Fat: **26.1g** Saturated Fat: **11.8g**; Trans Fat: **0g**
Protein: **67.3g**; Net Carbs: **8.7g**
Total Carbs: **9.8g**; Dietary Fiber: **1.1g**; Sugars: **7.2g**
Cholesterol: 202mg; Sodium: 572mg; Potassium: 113mg;
Vitamin A: 2%; **Vitamin C**: 49%; **Calcium**: 1%; **Iron**: 37%.

Ingredients:
- 3 pounds beef roast
- 1 onion, diced
- 6 cloves garlic, minced
- 1 green pepper, diced
- 3 tablespoons cumin
- 1 tablespoon oregano
- 1 teaspoon paprika
- 2 tablespoons chopped cilantro
- salt and pepper, to taste
- ½ cup water

Directions:
1. Toss together the cumin, oregano, paprika, cilantro, salt and pepper in a small bowl.
2. Rub the beef roast with half of the spices.

3. Put the roast into the slow cooker and add the diced onion, minced garlic and diced green pepper. Pour in ½ a cup of water.
4. Cover and cook on low for 8 hours. Remove the beef, shred it to bite-size pieces, then return it back into the slow cooker, along with the remaining spices and cook for another half an hour.

Kielbasa and Cabbage

Prep Time: **5 minutes;** Cook Time: **6-8 hours**
Serving Size: **343g;** Serves: **4**; Calories: **162**
Total Fat: **3g** Saturated Fat: **1g;** Trans Fat: **0g**
Protein: **12g;** Net Carbs: **13.7g**
Total Carbs: **21.3g;** Dietary Fiber: **7.6g;** Sugars: **11.6g**
Cholesterol: 25mg; Sodium: 384mg; Potassium: 176mg;
Vitamin A: 153%; **Vitamin C**: 219%; **Calcium**: 14%; **Iron**: 10%.

Ingredients:
- 2 links kielbasa, cut into 2-inch pieces
- 1 head green cabbage, roughly chopped
- 2-3 carrots, sliced
- caraway seeds, to taste
- ½ cup sauerkraut
- salt and pepper, to taste

Directions:

1. Place all the ingredients into the slow cooker and cook on low for 6 to 8 hours.

Butter Chicken

Prep Time: 10 minutes; Cook Time: 6-8 hours
Serving Size: **305g**; Serves: **4**; Calories: **412**
Total Fat: **27.8g** Saturated Fat: **24g**; Trans Fat: **0g**
Protein: **26.7g**; Net Carbs: **13.8g**
Total Carbs: **19.6g**; Dietary Fiber: **5.8g**; Sugars: **9.8g**
Cholesterol: 48mg; Sodium: 452mg; Potassium: 726mg;
Vitamin A: 8%; **Vitamin C**: 23%; **Calcium**: 3%; **Iron**: 20%.

Ingredients:
- 1 pound boneless, skinless chicken breast or chicken thighs
- 2 teaspoons coconut oil
- 1 medium onion, diced
- 4 cloves garlic, finely minced
- 1 teaspoon fresh ginger, finely minced
- 1 teaspoon cardamom
- ½ teaspoon salt
- 1 (14-ounce) can coconut milk
- 1 (6-ounce) can tomato paste
- juice from 1 lime

Directions:
1. Heat the coconut oil in a skillet or pan. Toss in the onion and sauté until it turns translucent. Add the

minced garlic, ginger, cardamom and salt. Sauté for 1 minute more.
2. Pour in the coconut milk and tomato paste and stir well.
3. Add in the chicken and cook on low for 6 to 8 hours.
4. Shred the chicken into bite-size pieces and serve with the sauce, drizzled with lime juice.

Moroccan Chicken

Prep Time: 15 minutes; Cook Time: 4-5 hours
Serving Size: **318g;** Serves: **4**; Calories: **299**
Total Fat: **4.4g** Saturated Fat: **0g**; Trans Fat: **0g**
Protein: **46.5g;** Net Carbs: **16.6g**
Total Carbs: **18g**; Dietary Fiber: **1.4g**; Sugars: **12.7g**
Cholesterol: 96mg; Sodium: 1103mg; Potassium: 197mg;
Vitamin A: 0%; **Vitamin C**: 15%; **Calcium**: 2%; **Iron**: 2%.

Ingredients:
- 2 pounds boneless, skinless chicken thighs, trimmed of excess fat
- ½ teaspoon salt
- 1 teaspoon paprika
- 1 teaspoon ground ginger
- 1 teaspoon ground cumin
- 1 teaspoon ground coriander
- ½ teaspoon ground cinnamon
- ½ teaspoon ground allspice
- ¼ teaspoon crushed fennel seeds

- 1 red onion, roughly chopped
- 3 cloves garlic, minced
- 1 cup pitted green olives
- ½ cup raisins
- ½ fresh lemon, thinly sliced

Directions:
1. Salt the chicken and set aside.
2. Stir the paprika, ginger, cumin, coriander, cinnamon, allspice and fennel seeds in a small bowl.
3. Layer the chopped onion, chicken, spices mix, minced garlic, raisins and lemon in the slow cooker in this order.
4. Cover and cook on low for 4 to 5 hours. Stir everything once towards the end.

Lemon Garlic Chicken

Prep Time: **10 minutes;** Cook Time: **4 hours**
Serving Size: **142g;** Serves: **4;** Calories: **189**
Total Fat: **6.3g** Saturated Fat: **1.7g;** Trans Fat: **0g**
Protein: **21.5g;** Net Carbs: **11.2g**
Total Carbs: **13g;** Dietary Fiber: **1.8g;** Sugars: **1.4g**
Cholesterol: 67mg; Sodium: 70mg; Potassium: 341mg;
Vitamin A: 1%; **Vitamin C**: 53%; **Calcium**: 7%; **Iron**: 9%.

Ingredients:
- 3 lemons, halved
- 3 heads garlic, halved
- 3 sprigs fresh rosemary
- 3 chicken leg quarters

- salt and pepper, to taste

Directions:
1. Place the lemon halves, garlic heads and rosemary into the slow cooker.
2. Put the chicken legs on top of that and season with salt and pepper to taste.
3. Cover and cook for 4 hours on high.
4. Let the chicken rest for about 10 minutes before serving.

Pineapple-Cranberry Pork Loin

Prep Time: 10 minutes; Cook Time: 8-10 hours
Serving Size: **316g**; Serves: **8**; Calories: **557**
Total Fat: **21.7g** Saturated Fat: **7.9g**; Trans Fat: **0g**
Protein: **64.4g**; Net Carbs: **8g**
Total Carbs: **21.5g**; Dietary Fiber: **1.4g**; Sugars: **19.1g**
Cholesterol: 182mg; Sodium: 140mg; Potassium: 961mg;
Vitamin A: 2%; **Vitamin C**: 12%; **Calcium**: 5%; **Iron**: 16%.

Ingredients:
- 4 pounds pork loin roast
- salt and pepper, to taste
- 1 (16-ounce) can crushed pineapple
- ¼ teaspoon nutmeg
- 1 can cranberry sauce

Directions:

1. Put all the ingredients into the slow cooker and cook on low for 8 to 10 hours.
2. Slice the pork and serve it topped with the sauce.

Crispy Slow Cooker Turkey

Prep Time: **5 minutes;** Cook Time: **7 hours**
Serving Size: **85g;** Serves: **4**; Calories: **110**
Total Fat: **5g** Saturated Fat: **1g;** Trans Fat: **0g**
Protein: **22g;** Net Carbs: **8g**
Total Carbs: **0g;** Dietary Fiber: **0g;** Sugars: **0g**
Cholesterol: **70mg;** Sodium: **75mg;** Potassium: **0mg;**
Vitamin A: 0%; **Vitamin C:** 0%; **Calcium:** 0%; **Iron:** 2%.

Ingredients:
- 4 turkey thighs, skin and bone on
- salt, to taste
- black pepper, to taste

Directions:
1. Place the turkey, skin-side up, into the slow cooker and season with salt and pepper to taste.
2. Cover and cook on low for 7 hours.
3. Cook with the lid slightly opened for the last hour if you want the skin to be crispier.

Balsamic Chicken

Prep Time: **5 minutes;** Cook Time: **4-6 hours**
Serving Size: **166g;** Serves: **4**; Calories: **196**
Total Fat: **7.5g** Saturated Fat: **2g;** Trans Fat: **0g**
Protein: **25.3g;** Net Carbs: **5g**
Total Carbs: **5.2g;** Dietary Fiber: **0.2g;** Sugars: **4.7g**

Cholesterol: 65mg; Sodium: 236mg; Potassium: 28mg; **Vitamin A**: 1%; **Vitamin C**: 13%; **Calcium**: 0%; **Iron**: 8%.

Ingredients:
- 1 tablespoon olive oil
- ½ cup balsamic vinegar
- 1 pound chicken breasts
- 1 teaspoon garlic powder
- 1 teaspoon basil
- ½ teaspoon salt
- ¼ cup chopped onion
- ¼ cup chopped pepper

Directions:
1. Grease the slow cooker with some olive oil, then pour in the balsamic vinegar.
2. Rub the chicken breasts with garlic powder, basil and salt.
3. Add the chicken into the slow cooker, add the chopped onion and pepper.
4. Cook on low for 4 to 6 hours.

Slow Cooker Kalua Pork

Prep Time: 15 minutes; Cook Time: 13-14 hours
Serving Size: **226g;** Serves: **8**; Calories: **577**
Total Fat: **45.8g** Saturated Fat: **15.9g;** Trans Fat: **0g**
Protein: **37.8g;** Net Carbs: **0g**
Total Carbs: **0g;** Dietary Fiber: **0g;** Sugars: **0g**
Cholesterol: 159mg; Sodium: 539mg; Potassium: 0mg;

Vitamin A: 0%; **Vitamin C**: 4%; **Calcium**: 0%; **Iron**: 12%.

Ingredients:
- 4 pounds boneless pork shoulder
- 2 teaspoon sea salt
- 1 ½ teaspoon garlic powder

Directions:
1. Dry the pork with paper towels and pierce it with a knife all over.
2. Rub the pork with salt and place it into the slow cooker.
3. Sprinkle with garlic powder, cover and cook for 12 hours on low. Turn once midway through cooking.
4. When done, shred the meat into bite-size pieces, return it into the slow cooker, pour 1 cup of water into the slow cooker and cook for 1 to 2 hours more.
5. Serve right away.

Apricot Slow Cooker Chicken

Prep Time: 15 minutes; Cook Time: 4-5 hours
Serving Size: **150g**; Serves: **8**; Calories: **235**
Total Fat: **1.1g** Saturated Fat: **0.3g**; Trans Fat: **0g**
Protein: **12.7g**; Net Carbs: **8g**
Total Carbs: **45.7g**; Dietary Fiber: **0.1g**; Sugars: **41.6g**
Cholesterol: 33mg; Sodium: 343mg; Potassium: 62mg;
Vitamin A: 0%; **Vitamin C**: 43%; **Calcium**: 0%; **Iron**: 2%.

Ingredients:
- 4 chicken breasts, boneless and skinless
- 1 (18-ounce) jar apricot preserves (no added sugar)
- ½ cup fresh lemon juice
- ½ cup water
- 1 envelope onion soup mix

Directions:
1. Put the chicken into the slow cooker.
2. In a small bowl, stir the preserves, lemon juice, water and onion soup mix. Pour it over the chicken.
3. Cook for 4 to 5 hours on low. Serve warm.

Shredded Puttanesca Chicken

Prep Time: **10 minutes**; Cook Time: **7 hours**
Serving Size: **295g**; Serves: **4**; Calories: **216**
Total Fat: **6.2g** Saturated Fat: **1g**; Trans Fat: **0g**
Protein: **34.8g**; Net Carbs: **2.8g**
Total Carbs: **3.7g**; Dietary Fiber: **0.9g**; Sugars: **1.5g**
Cholesterol: 85mg; Sodium: 707mg; Potassium: 127mg;
Vitamin A: 2%; **Vitamin C**: 11%; **Calcium**: 3%; **Iron**: 4%.

Ingredients:
- 4-5 chicken breasts
- 1 can whole tomatoes, roughly mashed
- 4 cloves garlic, minced
- ½ cup sliced Kalamata olives
- ¼ cup capers
- 1 tablespoon dried oregano

Directions:
1. Place all the ingredients into the slow cooker and cook on low for 7 hours.
2. When done, remove the chicken and shred it into bite-size pieces.
3. Serve the shredded chicken covered with the remaining sauce.

Sticky Honey Pecan Chicken

Prep Time: 15 minutes; Cook Time: 3-4 hours
Serving Size: **285g;** Serves: **4**; Calories: **556**
Total Fat: **25.5g** Saturated Fat: **3g**; Trans Fat: **0g**
Protein: **37.3g**; Net Carbs: **48.3g**
Total Carbs: **51.5g**; Dietary Fiber: **3.2g**; Sugars: **47.6g**
Cholesterol: 85mg; Sodium: 683mg; Potassium: 163mg;
Vitamin A: 0%; **Vitamin C**: 2%; **Calcium**: 3%; **Iron**: 6%.

Ingredients:
- 4 chicken breasts
- 1 teaspoon sea salt
- 2/3 cups honey
- 1 cup chopped pecans
- 3 cloves garlic, minced

Directions:
1. Season the chicken with salt and put it into the slow cooker.
2. Stir together the honey and minced garlic in a small bowl. Pour it over the chicken and sprinkle with chopped pecans.
3. Cover and cook for 3 to 4 hours on low.
4. Let the chicken rest for about 10 minutes before serving. Serve the breasts whole or shredded.

Pulled BBQ Chicken

Prep Time: **10 minutes**; Cook Time: **4 hours**
Serving Size: **280g**; Serves: **8**; Calories: **308**
Total Fat: **15.8g** Saturated Fat: **4.1g**; Trans Fat: **0g**
Protein: **30g**; Net Carbs: **8.7g**
Total Carbs: **11.6g**; Dietary Fiber: **2.9g**; Sugars: **7.6g**
Cholesterol: 106mg; Sodium: 860mg; Potassium: 231mg;
Vitamin A: 12%; **Vitamin C**: 16%; **Calcium**: 2%; **Iron**: 13%.

Ingredients:
- 3 pounds organic chicken breast
- 2 cups diced tomatoes
- 3 pitted dates
- 3 cloves garlic, minced
- 1 small yellow onion, peeled and quartered
- 3 tablespoons apple cider vinegar
- 2 teaspoons sea salt
- 6 ounces tomato paste
- 1 ½ tablespoons avocado oil

Directions:
1. Place the chicken into the slow cooker.
2. Put the remaining ingredients into a food processor and blend until well chopped. Pour the blend over the chicken, cover and cook for 4 hours on low.

3. When done, shred the chicken with two forks, return the meat into the slow cooker and stir well.
4. Serve warm.

Ranchero Chicken

Prep Time: **10 minutes;** Cook Time: **8 hours**
Serving Size: **374g;** Serves: **4;** Calories: **336**
Total Fat: **8.1g** Saturated Fat: **1.5g;** Trans Fat: **0g**
Protein: **49g;** Net Carbs: **9.9g**
Total Carbs: **14.2g;** Dietary Fiber: **4.3g;** Sugars: **8.6g**
Cholesterol: 160mg; Sodium: 386mg; Potassium: 413mg;
Vitamin A: 17%; **Vitamin C**: 24%; **Calcium**: 2%; **Iron**: 21%.

Ingredients:
- 1 (15-ounce) can diced tomatoes
- 1 (6-ounce) can tomato paste
- 3 tablespoons homemade taco seasoning
- 1 pound chicken breasts, boneless and skinless
- 1 pound chicken thighs, boneless and skinless
- salt and pepper, to taste

Directions:
1. Whisk the diced tomatoes, tomato paste and taco seasoning in the slow cooker.
2. Toss in the chicken and stir well. Season to taste.
3. Cook on low for 8 hours.
4. When done, shred the chicken with two forks and serve it in tacos, on tostadas or in enchiladas.

Mediterranean Salmon

Prep Time: **10 minutes**; Cook Time: **6 hours**
Serving Size: **227g**; Serves: **4**; Calories: **205**
Total Fat: **10.7g** Saturated Fat: **1.5g**; Trans Fat: **0g**
Protein: **23.1g**; Net Carbs: **4.6g**
Total Carbs: **6.1g**; Dietary Fiber: **1.5g**; Sugars: **1.8g**
Cholesterol: 50mg; Sodium: 253mg; Potassium: 684mg;
Vitamin A: 4%; **Vitamin C**: 105%; **Calcium**: 5%; **Iron**: 12%.

Ingredients:
- 1 pound salmon fillets
- ½ teaspoon salt, divided
- 1 teaspoon garlic powder, divided
- 1 teaspoon onion powder, divided
- 1 tablespoon olive oil, divided
- 3 cloves garlic, sliced
- ½ onion, sliced
- 1 zucchini, quartered and sliced
- 1 red bell pepper, julienned
- 1 tomato, chopped

Directions:
1. Spray an oval oven safe dish with cooking spray and put the salmon into the oval dish. Season with salt, garlic powder, onion powder and olive oil.
2. Add in the sliced garlic, onion, zucchini, pepper and tomato.

3. Cover the dish with a glass lid or aluminum foil. Place the dish into the slow cooker and cover with the lid of the slow cooker.
4. Cook for about 6 hours on low.

Pork and Squash Ragout

Prep Time: 15 minutes; Cook Time: 6-8 hours
Serving Size: **254g;** Serves: **4**; Calories: **225**
Total Fat: **8.1g** Saturated Fat: **3g**; Trans Fat: **0g**
Protein: **22.1g;** Net Carbs: **11.6g**
Total Carbs: **15.3g**; Dietary Fiber: **3.7g**; Sugars: **6.4g**
Cholesterol: 60mg; Sodium: 521mg; Potassium: 331mg;
Vitamin A: 104%; **Vitamin C**: 33%; **Calcium**: 5%; **Iron**: 15%.

Ingredients:
- 1 pound boneless pork loin, cut into 3/4-inch cubes
- 1 cup peeled cubed butternut squash
- 1 ½ cups chopped onions
- 2 carrots, peeled and sliced
- salt and black pepper, to taste

Directions:

1. Combine all the ingredients in the slow cooker, except for salt and pepper.
2. Cover and cook on low for 6 to 8 hours.
3. When done, season with salt and pepper. Serve warm.

Chipotle Pumpkin Chicken

Prep Time: 15 minutes; Cook Time: 6-7 hours
Serving Size: **320g**; Serves: **4**; Calories: **255**
Total Fat: **6g** Saturated Fat: **2.3g**; Trans Fat: **0g**
Protein: **39.4g**; Net Carbs: **7g**
Total Carbs: **9.7g**; Dietary Fiber: **2.7g**; Sugars: **3.5g**
Cholesterol: 98mg; Sodium: 71mg; Potassium: 178mg; **Vitamin A**: 248%; **Vitamin C**: 7%; **Calcium**: 4%; **Iron**: 9%.

Ingredients:
- 1.5 pounds chicken breasts
- 1 (15-ounce) can pure pumpkin puree
- 2 teaspoons chipotle powder
- ¼ cup minced roasted poblano pepper
- 1 teaspoon minced garlic
- 1 teaspoon onion powder
- ½ teaspoon cumin
- ¾ cup water

Directions:
1. Put the chicken and all the remaining ingredients into the slow cooker.
2. Stir well and cook on low for 6 to 7 hours.

Brussel Sprouts with Bacon and Chicken

Prep Time: **15 minutes;** Cook Time: **8 hours**
Serving Size: **525g;** Serves: **4;** Calories: **546**
Total Fat: **28.1g** Saturated Fat: **8.2g;** Trans Fat: **0g**
Protein: **35.5g;** Net Carbs: **30.3g**
Total Carbs: **37.1g;** Dietary Fiber: **6.8g;** Sugars: **24.2g**
Cholesterol: 147mg; Sodium: 350mg; Potassium: 782mg;
Vitamin A: 334%; **Vitamin C**: 168%; **Calcium**: 12%; **Iron**: 25%.

Ingredients:
- 1 pound brussels sprouts, ends trimmed
- 1 pound large carrots, peeled and sliced into 1/2" circles
- 2 tablespoons maple syrup
- 1 sweet onion, chopped
- 3 slices bacon, chopped
- 1 ½ pounds bone-in chicken with skin
- 12 ounces apple cider

Directions:
1. Put the brussels sprouts, sliced carrots and maple syrup into the slow cooker.
2. Toss the onion and bacon in a skillet and sauté until the onion starts to brown. Transfer the onions and bacon into the slow cooker and stir well.

3. Place the chicken into the same skillet and cook it in the bacon drippings for about 5 minutes per side. Transfer the chicken into the slow cooker as well.
4. Pour the apple cider into the slow cooker, cover and cook on low for 8 hours.

Shredded Taco Meat

Prep Time: 15 minutes; Cook Time: 4-6 hours
Serving Size: **421g**; Serves: **4**; Calories: **533**
Total Fat: **24.1g** Saturated Fat: **10.7g**; Trans Fat: **0g**
Protein: **63.3g**; Net Carbs: **7.8g**
Total Carbs: **10.7g**; Dietary Fiber: **2.9g**; Sugars: **6.1g**
Cholesterol: 161mg; Sodium: 417mg; Potassium: 118mg;
Vitamin A: 10%; **Vitamin C**: 183%; **Calcium**: 2%; **Iron**: 38%.

Ingredients:
- 2 pounds flank steak
- 2 red bell peppers, chopped
- 1 large red onion, chopped
- 1 tube cilantro, chopped
- 2 tablespoons garlic, minced
- 2 tablespoons chili pepper, chopped
- 1 (15-ounce) can diced tomatoes
- ½ cup red wine vinegar
- 1 tablespoon ground cumin

Directions:

1. Place all the ingredients into the slow cooker, stir well and cook on high for 4 to 6 hours.
2. When done, remove the meat from the slow cooker and shred it.
3. Serve the shredded meat with the remaining sauce.

Pineapple Pork Ribs

Prep Time: 15 minutes; Cook Time: 7-8 hours
Serving Size: **713g**; Serves: **4**; Calories: **702**
Total Fat: **31.2g** Saturated Fat: **0g;** Trans Fat: **0g**
Protein: **63.1g;** Net Carbs: **30.2g**
Total Carbs: **35.6g**; Dietary Fiber: **5.4g**; Sugars: **17.2g**
Cholesterol: 0mg; Sodium: 414mg; Potassium: 590mg; **Vitamin A**: 4%; **Vitamin C**: 192%; **Calcium**: 2%; **Iron**: 28%.

Ingredients:
- 3 pounds baby back pork ribs
- 6 medium sized tomatoes, chopped
- 4 cups chopped, fresh pineapple
- 1 cup chopped green onion
- 2 tablespoons dried basil
- 2 tablespoons dried rosemary
- 1 teaspoon sea salt

Directions:
1. Put all the ingredients into the slow cooker and cook on low for 7 to 8 hours.

2. Serve right away.

Paleo Turkey Meatballs

Prep Time: **20 minutes;** Cook Time: **6 hours**
Serving Size: **90g;** Serves: **20**; Calories: **104**
Total Fat: **5.4g** Saturated Fat: **0.9g;** Trans Fat: **0g**
Protein: **10.2g;** Net Carbs: **3.8g**
Total Carbs: **5.3g;** Dietary Fiber: **1.5g;** Sugars: **2.9g**
Cholesterol: 46mg; Sodium: 248mg; Potassium: 105mg;
Vitamin A: 5%; **Vitamin C**: 4%; **Calcium**: 2%; **Iron**: 6%.

Ingredients:
- 1 pound ground turkey
- 1 pound turkey sausage, ground or in casing
- 1 teaspoon basil
- ½ teaspoon oregano
- ½ teaspoon rosemary
- ½ teaspoon thyme
- ½ teaspoon onion powder
- ½ teaspoon garlic powder
- 1 teaspoon salt
- ½ cup almond meal
- 1 egg, beaten
- 24 ounces crushed tomatoes
- ½ large onion, quartered
- 2 cloves garlic, crushed
- 2 tablespoons red wine vinegar

Directions:

1. Stir together the ground turkey and turkey sausage in a large bowl.
2. In a smaller bowl, mix the basil, oregano, rosemary, thyme, onion powder, garlic powder, salt and almond meal. Add the spices to the meat.
3. Knead the meaty dough with your hands, add the egg and knead until well incorporated.
4. Form about 20 meatballs with your hands.
5. Add the meatballs into a greased, heated skillet and cook them about 1 minute per side.
6. Transfer the meatballs into the slow cooker. Add the tomatoes, quartered onion, crushed garlic and red wine vinegar.
7. Cook for 5 to 6 hours on low.

BBQ Pork Spare Ribs

Prep Time: **5 minutes;** Cook Time: **6-8 hours**
Serving Size: **278g;** Serves: **8**; Calories: **469**
Total Fat: **28.1g** Saturated Fat: **12.1g**; Trans Fat: **0g**
Protein: **41g;** Net Carbs: **9.8g**
Total Carbs: **11.5g**; Dietary Fiber: **1.7g**; Sugars: **8.6g**
Cholesterol: 111mg; Sodium: 516mg; Potassium: 237mg;
Vitamin A: 4%; **Vitamin C**: 5%; **Calcium**: 0%; **Iron**: 14%.

Ingredients:

- 4 pounds pork spare ribs
- salt, to taste
- 2 (6-ounce) cans tomato paste
- 1.5 cup water
- 1 large onion, diced
- 4 tablespoons balsamic vinegar
- 2 tablespoons white vinegar
- 2 tablespoons raw honey
- 2 teaspoons garlic power
- 1 teaspoon cumin

Directions:
1. Rub the ribs with salt. Place all the remaining ingredients into the slow cooker and stir well.
2. Add the chicken and coat it in the sauce.
3. Cook on low for 6 to 8 hours.

Persian Lamb and Eggplant Stew
Prep Time: **15 minutes;** Cook Time: **10 hours**
Serving Size: **510g;** Serves: **4**; Calories: **378**
Total Fat: **20.2g** Saturated Fat: **7.6g;** Trans Fat: **0g**
Protein: **24.7g;** Net Carbs: **20g**
Total Carbs: **28g;** Dietary Fiber: **8g;** Sugars: **13.8g**
Cholesterol: 0mg; Sodium: 695mg; Potassium: 270mg; **Vitamin A**: 18%; **Vitamin C**: 39%; **Calcium**: 7%; **Iron**: 6%.

Ingredients:
- 1 pound lean boneless cubed lamb
- 1 pound peeled diced eggplant

- 2 cups diced onion
- 1 tablespoon olive oil
- salt and black pepper, to taste
- 1 teaspoon cinnamon
- 1 teaspoon turmeric
- 5 garlic cloves, minced
- 28 ounces canned diced tomatoes (with juice)

Directions:
1. Grease a skillet with olive oil and add the onion and lamb. Cook until the lamb is browned.
2. Transfer the lamb into the slow cooker and add all the remaining ingredients.
3. Cover and cook on low for 10 hours.

Chicken with Tomatoes

Prep Time: **15 minutes;** Cook Time: **6 hours**
Serving Size: **245g;** Serves: **4;** Calories: **195**
Total Fat: **6.7g** Saturated Fat: **2.1g;** Trans Fat: **0g**
Protein: **25.1g;** Net Carbs: **5.8g**
Total Carbs: **7.7g;** Dietary Fiber: **1.9g;** Sugars: **3.5g**
Cholesterol: 71mg; Sodium: 406mg; Potassium: 63mg;
Vitamin A: 16%; **Vitamin C**: 24%; **Calcium**: 3%; **Iron**: 6%.

Ingredients:
- 8 ounces chicken half breasts
- 8 ounces boneless chicken breasts
- 6 cloves garlic, minced
- 2 shallots, sliced

- 1 teaspoon dried thyme
- 1 teaspoon fennel seeds
- 1 teaspoon ground pepper
- 1 bay leaf
- 1/3 cup red wine vinegar
- 1 (14-ounce) can diced tomatoes
- ¼ cup finely chopped fresh parsley

Directions:
1. Grease a skillet with olive oil spray. Toss in the shallots and sauté for 3 to 6 minutes.
2. Add the garlic, thyme, fennel seeds, ground pepper and bay leaf. Stir for 1 minute.
3. Pour in the vinegar and boil for 2 minutes.
4. Add the diced tomatoes and stir.
5. Place the chicken into the slow cooker and add the tomato mixture.
6. Cover and cook on low for 6 hours.
7. Before serving, remove the bay leaf and serve with fresh parsley.

Spicy Beef Curry Stew

Prep Time: 15 minutes; Cook Time: 6-8 hours
Serving Size: **311g**; Serves: **4**; Calories: **312**
Total Fat: **18.8g** Saturated Fat: **6.6g**; Trans Fat: **0g**
Protein: **27.2g**; Net Carbs: **6g**
Total Carbs: **8.5g**; Dietary Fiber: **2.5g**; Sugars: **4.8g**

Cholesterol: 80mg; Sodium: 471mg; Potassium: 86mg; **Vitamin A**: 9%; **Vitamin C**: 20%; **Calcium**: 3%; **Iron**: 3%.

Ingredients:
- 1 tablespoon olive oil
- 1 pound beef stew meat
- salt and pepper, to taste
- 2 cloves garlic, minced
- 1 teaspoon chopped fresh ginger
- 1 jalapeno pepper, fresh, diced
- 1 tablespoon curry powder
- 1 (14.5-ounce) can diced tomatoes with juice
- 1 onion, sliced and quartered
- 1 cup beef broth

Directions:
1. Heat the olive oil in a skillet and add the beef. Brown the meat on all sides and season with salt and pepper to taste.
2. Add the garlic, ginger and jalapeno pepper and cook for 2 more minutes. Season with curry powder, then pour in the diced tomatoes with juice.
3. Layer the sliced onion in the slow cooker and top it with beef and the mixture from the skillet. Pour in the beef broth.
4. Cover and cook on low for 6 to 8 hours.

Cuban Chicken

Prep Time: 15 minutes; Cook Time: 6-8 hours
Serving Size: **233g;** Serves: **4**; Calories: **158**
Total Fat: **2.1g** Saturated Fat: **1g**; Trans Fat: **0g**
Protein: **20.5g**; Net Carbs: **11.2g**
Total Carbs: **15.7g**; Dietary Fiber: **4.5g**; Sugars: **8.5g**
Cholesterol: 50mg; Sodium: 1007mg; Potassium: 614mg;
Vitamin A: 15%; **Vitamin C**: 52%; **Calcium**: 1%; **Iron**: 14%.

Ingredients:
- 1 pound boneless, skinless chicken breasts
- 1 (4 ½-ounce) can diced tomatoes
- 1 tablespoon cumin
- 1 ½ teaspoon dried oregano
- 4 cloves garlic, minced
- 1 green pepper, diced
- 1 (8-ounce) can tomato paste

Directions:
1. Stir the diced tomatoes, cumin, oregano, garlic, green pepper and tomato paste together in the slow cooker. Place the chicken breasts on top and cook on low for 6 to 8 hours.
2. Shred the chicken into bite-size pieces before serving.

Middle Eastern Ribs

Prep Time: **5 minutes**; Cook Time: **8 hours**
Serving Size: **225g**; Serves: **8**; Calories: **614**
Total Fat: **39.8g** Saturated Fat: **14.2g**; Trans Fat: **0g**
Protein: **59.6g**; Net Carbs: **0g**
Total Carbs: **0g**; Dietary Fiber: **0g**; Sugars: **0g**
Cholesterol: 232mg; Sodium: 326mg; Potassium: 648mg;
Vitamin A: 0%; **Vitamin C**: 0%; **Calcium**: 8%; **Iron**: 17%.

Ingredients:
- 4 pounds ribs
- 1 tablespoon cumin
- 1 tablespoon onion powder
- 1 tablespoon garlic powder
- 1 teaspoon paprika
- 1 teaspoon salt
- ½ teaspoon cayenne
- 1 teaspoon cinnamon

Directions:
1. Whisk together the spices in a small bowl and set aside.
2. Rub the ribs with the spice mixture and place them into the slow cooker.
3. Cook on low for at least 8 hours.

Mongolian Beef

Prep Time: **5 minutes;** Cook Time: **4-6 hours**
Serving Size: **232g;** Serves: **4;** Calories: **379**
Total Fat: **22g** Saturated Fat: **10.5g;** Trans Fat: **0g**
Protein: **28g;** Net Carbs: **18.6g**
Total Carbs: **19g;** Dietary Fiber: **0.4g;** Sugars: **17.7g**
Cholesterol: 97mg; Sodium: 743mg; Potassium: 301mg;
Vitamin A: 1%; **Vitamin C:** 3%; **Calcium:** 0%; **Iron:** 14%.

Ingredients:
- 1 pound beef steak, thinly sliced
- ½ teaspoon sea salt
- 1/3 cup green onion, chopped
- 1 tablespoon minced fresh garlic
- 1 tablespoon fresh ginger, chopped
- 1 ½ cups bone broth
- ¼ cup raw honey
- 3 tablespoons apple cider vinegar
- 1 teaspoon fish sauce
- ¼ teaspoon garlic powder

Directions:
1. Place the beef slices into the slow cooker and season with salt.
2. Add the green onion, garlic and ginger.
3. Add the bone broth, honey, apple cider vinegar, fish sauce and garlic into a blender and blend.

4. Pour the mixture over the steak, cover and cook on low for 4 to 6 hours.

Korean Short Ribs

Prep Time: **15 minutes**; Cook Time: **9 hours**
Serving Size: **190g**; Serves: **8**; Calories: **562**
Total Fat: **50.4g** Saturated Fat: **22.1g**; Trans Fat: **0g**
Protein: **20.3g**; Net Carbs: **3.7g**
Total Carbs: **4.7g;** Dietary Fiber: **1g**; Sugars: **1.6g**
Cholesterol: 105mg; Sodium: 99mg; Potassium: 97mg; **Vitamin A**: 52%; **Vitamin C**: 7%; **Calcium**: 4%; **Iron**: 13%.

Ingredients:
- 2.5 pounds beef short ribs, cut
- 2 carrots, chopped
- 1 large daikon radish, cubed
- ½ Asian pear, cored and chopped
- ⅓ cup bone broth
- ¼ cup coconuts aminos
- 2 garlic cloves, minced
- 1 tablespoon ginger, minced
- 1 teaspoon fish sauce
- 1 teaspoon rice vinegar
- 3 green onions, chopped

Directions:
1. Season the ribs with some salt and pepper and place them into the slow cooker.
2. Add the carrots and daikon radish.

3. Place the Asian pear into a food processor and blend until smooth.
4. In a medium bowl, stir together the blended pear, bone broth, coconut aminos, minced garlic, ginger, fish sauce and rice vinegar. Pour the mixture over the ribs in the slow cooker.
5. Cook for 9 hours on low and serve with the chopped green onions.

Moroccan Chicken

Prep Time: **15 minutes;** Cook Time: **5 hours**
Serving Size: **480g;** Serves: **4**; Calories: **603**
Total Fat: **16.7g** Saturated Fat: **3.1g;** Trans Fat: **0g**
Protein: **98.3g;** Net Carbs: **3.7g**
Total Carbs: **3.6g;** Dietary Fiber: **0.9g;** Sugars: **2.9g**
Cholesterol: 260mg; Sodium: 870mg; Potassium: 669mg;
Vitamin A: 1%; **Vitamin C**: 28%; **Calcium**: 6%; **Iron**: 18%.

Ingredients:
- ½ cup water
- ½ cup juice from lemon and zest
- 1 teaspoon paprika
- 1 teaspoon ground cumin
- 1 teaspoon ground ginger
- ½ teaspoon cinnamon
- 3 pounds chicken
- 2 teaspoons minced garlic

- 1 small onion, minced
- ½ cup sliced green olives
- ½ cup sliced black olives

Directions:
1. Put all the ingredients into the slow cooker and cook on low for 4 ½ to 5 hours.

Lemon Dill Halibut

Prep Time: **5 minutes**; Cook Time: **2 hours**
Serving Size: **185g**; Serves: **2**; Calories: **237**
Total Fat: **10.9g** Saturated Fat: **1.6g**; Trans Fat: **0g**
Protein: **35.3g**; Net Carbs: **0.5g**
Total Carbs: **0.5g**; Dietary Fiber: **0g**; Sugars: **0.2g**
Cholesterol: 55mg; Sodium: 94mg; Potassium: 773mg;
Vitamin A: 0%; **Vitamin C**: 3%; **Calcium**: 0%; **Iron**: 0%.

Ingredients:
- 12 ounces wild Alaska seafood halibut
- salt and pepper, to taste
- 1 tablespoon fresh lemon juice
- 1 tablespoon olive oil
- 1 ½ teaspoon dried dill

Directions:
1. Place the halibut onto a large piece of non-stick foil and season it with salt and pepper.
2. Stir together the lemon juice, olive oil and dill in a small bowl. Drizzle over the fish.

3. Bring the edges of the foil up and crimp them loosely together.
4. Place the foil package into the slow cooker and cook on high for 2 hours.
5. Carefully open the packet and let the steam out. The fish should be very tender and flaky. Serve it drizzled with some more fresh lemon juice.

Honey-Poached Salmon

Prep Time: **20 minutes;** Cook Time: **1 hour**
Serving Size: **465g;** Serves: **4**; Calories: **466**
Total Fat: **15.8g** Saturated Fat: **3.5g;** Trans Fat: **0g**
Protein: **42.8g;** Net Carbs: **36.4g**
Total Carbs: **40.7g;** Dietary Fiber: **4.3g;** Sugars: **30.2g**
Cholesterol: 36mg; Sodium: 131mg; Potassium: 718mg;
Vitamin A: 10%; **Vitamin C**: 86%; **Calcium**: 7%; **Iron**: 4%.

Ingredients:
- 3 cups water
- 1 tablespoon raw honey
- 2 teaspoon whole allspice berries
- 4 (6-ounce) wild salmon fillets
- 4 thin lemon slices
- 1 large fennel bulb, trimmed of fronds and thinly sliced
- ½ cup thinly sliced red onion
- 2 oranges, peeled and thinly slices

- ¼ cup pomegranate arils
- 2 tablespoons chopped fresh mint
- 1 tablespoon olive oil
- 1 tablespoon white wine vinegar

Directions:
1. Stir water and honey in the slow cooker. Season with allspice berries and cook covered for 30 minutes on high.
2. Add in the salmon fillets and lemon slices. Cover and cook for another 20 to 30 minutes.
3. In the meantime, prepare the salad. Mix the fennel and red onion in a large bowl and top with thin orange slices, along with all its juices. Add the pomegranate arils, fresh mint, olive oil and white wine vinegar.
4. When cooked, serve the salmon with the salad.

Veggie Spaghetti

Prep Time: **10 minutes;** Cook Time: **4 hours**
Serving Size: **220g;** Serves: **8;** Calories: **217**
Total Fat: **14.3g** Saturated Fat: **5g;** Trans Fat: **0g**
Protein: **11.9g;** Net Carbs: **8.7g**
Total Carbs: **11.5g;** Dietary Fiber: **2.8g;** Sugars: **4.4g**
Cholesterol: 30mg; Sodium: 822mg; Potassium: 509mg;
Vitamin A: 5%; **Vitamin C**: 175%; **Calcium**: 6%; **Iron**: 14%.

Ingredients:
- 5 links Italian sausage
- 1 cup grape tomatoes
- 3 cloves garlic, minced
- 1 teaspoon Italian spice
- salt and pepper, to taste
- 1 teaspoon dried onion
- 4 cups shredded cabbage
- 3 sweet bell peppers, thinly sliced
- 2 small zucchini made into noodles

Directions:
1. Remove the casings from the Italian sausage links and chop them into small pieces.
2. Place all the ingredients into the slow cooker and stir well.
3. Cook for 8 hours on low or 4 hours on high. Stir well before serving.

Spicy Ginger Lime Wings

Prep Time: 10 minutes; Cook Time: 6-7 hours
Serving Size: **194g;** Serves: **6**; Calories: **546**
Total Fat: **34g** Saturated Fat: **9.2g**; Trans Fat: **0g**
Protein: **39.7g**; Net Carbs: **17.4g**
Total Carbs: **18.1g**; Dietary Fiber: **0.7g**; Sugars: **10.2g**
Cholesterol: 122mg; Sodium: 126mg; Potassium: 297mg;
Vitamin A: 4%; **Vitamin C**: 7%; **Calcium**: 5%; **Iron**: 14%.

Ingredients:

- 2 pounds chicken wings
- ¼ cup coconut aminos
- ¼ cup balsamic vinegar
- 3 tablespoons honey
- 4 cloves garlic, minced
- ½ teaspoon cayenne chili powder
- 2 teaspoons fresh grated ginger
- 3 tablespoons lime juice
- zest of 1 lime
- 2 teaspoons tapioca starch
- 2 teaspoons sesame seeds
- 2 tablespoons chopped chives

Directions:
1. Stir together the coconut aminos, vinegar, honey, minced garlic, cayenne chili powder, ginger, lime juice and zest in a large bowl.
2. Put the chicken wings into the slow cooker and pour in the sauce. Stir well.
3. Cover and cook for 6 to 7 hours on low.
4. Right before it is done, whisk together the tapioca starch and 1 tablespoon of water in a small bowl. Pour this mixture into the slow cooker and stir well.
5. Cover and cook for another 10 minutes or so, until the sauce thickens.
6. Serve right away, sprinkled with sesame seeds and chopped chives.

Squash and Ground Beef Curry
Prep Time: 10 minutes; Cook Time: 4-6 hours

Serving Size: **1267g;** Serves: **4**; Calories: **571**
Total Fat: **33.4g** Saturated Fat: **21.6g**; Trans Fat: **0g**
Protein: **45.2g**; Net Carbs: **22.2g**
Total Carbs: **30.3g**; Dietary Fiber: **8.1g**; Sugars: **3.9g**
Cholesterol: 120mg; Sodium: 154mg; Potassium: 544mg;
Vitamin A: 290%; **Vitamin C**: 42%; **Calcium**: 42%; **Iron**: 49%.

Ingredients:
- 2 pounds ground beef
- 1 whole acorn squash, cubed
- 13 ½ ounces coconut milk
- 15 ounces pumpkin puree
- 1 ½ cup water
- 1 ½ tablespoon ginger root, peeled and diced
- 5 cloves garlic
- 1 whole lemon, quartered
- ½ tablespoon garlic powder
- ½ tablespoon onion powder
- 1 teaspoon dried cilantro
- 1 teaspoon dried basil
- 1 teaspoon ground cinnamon
- ½ teaspoon ground ginger
- ¼ teaspoon ground cloves

Directions:
1. Break up the beef into tiny pieces and put it, along with all the other ingredients, into the slow cooker.
2. Cover and cook for 4 to 6 hours on low.
3. Before serving, break up the chunks of ground beef.

Easy Sausage Casserole

Prep Time: **10 minutes;** Cook Time: **5 hours**
Serving Size: **388g;** Serves: **4**; Calories: **516**
Total Fat: **34.5g** Saturated Fat: **11.9g;** Trans Fat: **0g**
Protein: **26.6g;** Net Carbs: **21.9g**
Total Carbs: **25.8g;** Dietary Fiber: **3.9g;** Sugars: **10.3g**
Cholesterol: 71mg; Sodium: 1787mg; Potassium: 958mg;
Vitamin A: 123%; **Vitamin C**: 44%; **Calcium**: 11%; **Iron**: 25%.

Ingredients:
- 6 large sausages, sliced
- 1 large onion, peeled and diced
- 1 medium zucchini, diced
- 2 large carrots, sliced
- 2 large leeks, sliced
- 1 pound tinned tomatoes
- 1 tablespoon parsley
- 1 tablespoon Italian seasoning

Directions:
1. Layer the sausages on the bottom of the slow cooker. Add the vegetables and the seasoning and stir well.
2. Cook on low for 5 hours.

Chicken Tikka Masala

Prep Time: **5 minutes**; Cook Time: **6 hours**
Serving Size: **836g**; Serves: **2**; Calories: **511**
Total Fat: **10.4g** Saturated Fat: **5g**; Trans Fat: **0g**
Protein: **57.9g**; Net Carbs: **2g**
Total Carbs: **11.5g**; Dietary Fiber: **9.5g**; Sugars: **24.6g**
Cholesterol: 131mg; Sodium: 1653mg; Potassium: 295mg;
Vitamin A: 47%; **Vitamin C**: 76%; **Calcium**: 7%; **Iron**: 39%.

Ingredients:

- 1 pound chicken breast or thighs, cut into bite-sized pieces
- 1 large onion, diced
- 1 teaspoon minced garlic
- 1 teaspoon garam masala
- 2 teaspoons paprika
- 28 ounces organic crushed tomatoes
- 1 teaspoon turmeric
- 1 teaspoon sea salt
- 2 tablespoons tomato paste
- ½ teaspoon cinnamon
- 1 cup full-fat coconut milk

Directions:

1. Put all the ingredients except for the coconut milk into the slow cooker. Stir well and cook for 6 hours on low.
2. Half an hour before it is done, pour in the coconut milk as well. Stir well.

Pork Ribs in Spicy Adobo Sauce

Prep Time: **25 minutes**; Cook Time: **4 hours**
Serving Size: **385g**; Serves: **4**; Calories: **676**
Total Fat: **43.5g** Saturated Fat: **14.7g**; Trans Fat: **0g**
Protein: **60.8g**; Net Carbs: **5.9g**
Total Carbs: **7.8g**; Dietary Fiber: **1.9g**; Sugars: **5.1g**
Cholesterol: 232mg; Sodium: 303mg; Potassium: 874mg;
Vitamin A: 3%; **Vitamin C**: 24%; **Calcium**: 12%; **Iron**: 24%.

Ingredients:
- 1 tablespoon olive oil
- 2 pounds pork ribs, separated into individual ribs
- 1 large onion, sliced into half moons
- 1 tablespoon garlic, minced
- 1 tablespoon smoked paprika
- 2 teaspoons fresh oregano
- 1 canned chipotle chili, minced
- 2 cups canned chopped tomatoes with the liquid
- 1 tablespoon red wine vinegar

Directions:
1. Heat the olive oil in a skillet and toss in the onion. Sauté until it turns translucent, then add the minced garlic and cook 1 minute more.

2. Season with paprika, oregano and chipotle chili. Cook for 3 minutes, then transfer everything into a slow cooker.
3. Add the tomatoes, red wine vinegar and pork ribs. Cook on low for 6 to 8 hours or on high for 4 hours.

Tuscan Chicken

Prep Time: **5 minutes;** Cook Time: **4-6 hours**
Serving Size: **440g;** Serves: **4**; Calories: **231**
Total Fat: **3.6g** Saturated Fat: **1g;** Trans Fat: **0g**
Protein: **36.5g;** Net Carbs: **8.5g**
Total Carbs: **12.3g;** Dietary Fiber: **3.8g;** Sugars: **6g**
Cholesterol: 85mg; Sodium: 970mg; Potassium: 505mg;
Vitamin A: 3%; **Vitamin C**: 13%; **Calcium**: 4%; **Iron**: 9%.

Ingredients:
- 4 chicken breasts, boneless and skinless
- 2 (15-ounce) cans fire-roasted tomatoes, undrained
- 1 cup sliced mushrooms
- 1 tablespoon minced garlic
- ½ white onion, thinly sliced
- 1 teaspoon Italian seasoning
- ½ teaspoon salt
- handful basil leaves, thinly sliced

Directions:

1. Stir the tomatoes, mushrooms, garlic, onion, seasoning, salt and basil in a medium bowl.
2. Layer the chicken breasts on the bottom of the slow cooker and add the tomato mixture.
3. Cover and let it cook on low for 4 to 6 hours.

Mushroom Chicken

Prep Time: 20 minutes; Cook Time: 3-4 hours
Serving Size: **257g;** Serves: **4**; Calories: **265**
Total Fat: **9g** Saturated Fat: **3g**; Trans Fat: **0g**
Protein: **36.5g;** Net Carbs: **6.5g**
Total Carbs: **8.1g;** Dietary Fiber: **1.6g**; Sugars: **2.4g**
Cholesterol: 120mg; Sodium: 792mg; Potassium: 253mg;
Vitamin A: 0%; **Vitamin C**: 6%; **Calcium**: 1%; **Iron**: 4%.

Ingredients:
- 4 (6-ounce) chicken breast halves, boneless and skinless
- 1 envelope onion mushroom soup mix
- 1 cup water
- ½ pound sliced baby Portobello mushrooms
- 1 medium onion, chopped
- 4 garlic cloves, minced

Directions:
1. Put the chicken, soup mix, water, mushrooms, onion and garlic into the slow cooker.

2. Cover and cook on low for 3 to 4 hours.

Sweet and Spicy Chicken Legs

Prep Time: **10 minutes;** Cook Time: **6 hours**
Serving Size: **374g;** Serves: **4;** Calories: **374**
Total Fat: **21.4g** Saturated Fat: **5.5g;** Trans Fat: **0g**
Protein: **18.8g;** Net Carbs: **24.1g**
Total Carbs: **29g;** Dietary Fiber: **4.9g;** Sugars: **19.8g**
Cholesterol: 79mg; Sodium: 644mg; Potassium: 152mg;
Vitamin A: 17%; **Vitamin C**: 32%; **Calcium**: 8%; **Iron**: 12%.

Ingredients:
- 2 teaspoons ground cumin
- ½ teaspoon ground cinnamon
- salt and pepper, to taste
- 4 chicken leg quarters
- 1 tablespoon olive oil
- 1 medium yellow onion, cut into 1/2-inch wedges
- 3 cloves garlic, minced
- 3-inch piece peeled fresh ginger, sliced into rounds
- 1 (28-ounce) ounce diced tomatoes, liquid included
- ½ cup raisins

Directions:

1. Mix the cumin, cinnamon, salt and pepper in zip-top bag. Add the chicken leg quarters and coat them with the spice mixture.
2. Heat the olive oil in a skillet and cook the chicken for about 2 to 4 minutes per side, until golden brown.
3. Place the onion, garlic and ginger into the slow cooker and add the chicken. Cover with tomatoes and raisins.
4. Cover and cook on low for 6 hours.

Desserts & Snacks

Unsweetened Pear Applesauce

Prep Time: 10 minutes; Cook Time: 6-8 hours
Serving Size: **206g;** Serves: **8**; Calories: **108**
Total Fat: **0.1g** Saturated Fat: **0g**; Trans Fat: **0g**
Protein: **0.3g**; Net Carbs: **22.7g**
Total Carbs: **29g**; Dietary Fiber: **6.3g**; Sugars: **20.7g**
Cholesterol: **0mg**; Sodium: **2mg**; Potassium: **244mg**;
Vitamin A: 0%; **Vitamin C**: 48%; **Calcium**: 1%; **Iron**: 47%.

Ingredients:
- 6 ripe apples, cored, peeled and chopped
- 4 ripe pears, peeled and chopped
- 1 teaspoon ground cinnamon
- ½ teaspoon ground nutmeg

- 1 teaspoon juice from lemon
- ¼ cup water

Directions:
1. Put all the ingredients into the slow cooker and stir well.
2. Cook on low for 6 to 8 hours.
3. You can store it in the refrigerator for up to 4 days.

Classic Homemade Applesauce

Prep Time: **10 minutes;** Cook Time: **9 hours**
Serving Size: **226g;** Serves: **8**; Calories: **102**
Total Fat: **0g** Saturated Fat: **0g;** Trans Fat: **0g**
Protein: **0g;** Net Carbs: **21.8g**
Total Carbs: **28.1g**; Dietary Fiber: **6.3g**; Sugars: **21.8g**
Cholesterol: **0mg;** Sodium: **1mg;** Potassium: **253mg;**
Vitamin A: 0%; **Vitamin C**: 71%; **Calcium**: 0%; **Iron**: 79%.

Ingredients:
- 3 ½ pounds apples
- ½ teaspoon ground cinnamon
- 1 cup water

Directions:
1. Peel, core and quarter the apples.
2. Put all the ingredients into the slow cooker and cook on low for 8 to 9 hours.

Apple-Cranberry Dessert

Prep Time: **10 minutes;** Cook Time: **4 hours**
Serving Size: **140g;** Serves: **8**; Calories: **223**
Total Fat: **0.1g** Saturated Fat: **0g**; Trans Fat: **0g**
Protein: **0.4g;** Net Carbs: **54.1g**
Total Carbs: **55.9g;** Dietary Fiber: **1.8g**; Sugars: **45.2g**
Cholesterol: **0mg;** Sodium: **54mg;** Potassium: **83mg;**
Vitamin A: 00%; **Vitamin C**: 4%; **Calcium**: 1%; **Iron**: 3%.

Ingredients:
- 21 ounces apple pie filling (no sugar added)
- 16 ounces fresh cranberries, finely mashed
- ½ cup raisins
- 1 ½ tablespoons ground cinnamon
- ¼ teaspoon ground nutmeg

Directions:
1. Grease the slow cooker with cooking spray.
2. In a medium bowl, stir together the apple pie filling, cranberries, raisins, cinnamon and nutmeg.
3. Transfer into the slow cooker, cover and cook on low for 4 hours.

Cinnamon Poached Pears

Prep Time: 10 minutes; Cook Time: 90 minutes
Serving Size: **166g**; Serves: **9**; Calories: **96**
Total Fat: **0.2g** Saturated Fat: **0g**; Trans Fat: **0g**
Protein: **0.6g**; Net Carbs: **20.2g**
Total Carbs: **25.3g**; Dietary Fiber: **5.1g**; Sugars: **16.2g**
Cholesterol: **0mg**; Sodium: **2mg**; Potassium: **193mg**;
Vitamin A: 1%; **Vitamin C**: 12%; **Calcium**: 1%; **Iron**: 2%.

Ingredients:
- 9 firm, under-ripe pears
- 1 cinnamon stick
- ¾ cup Monk Fruit In The Raw

Directions:
1. Remove the cores from the bottom ends of the pears while leaving the stem intact. Cut off the bottoms so they sit flat.
2. Place the cinnamon stick and monk fruit into the slow cooker.
3. Place all of the pears cut side down into the slow cooker and cook on high for 90 minutes.
4. When done, transfer the pears onto individual serving plates.

Pumpkin Butter

Prep Time: **10 minutes**; Cook Time: **6 hours**
Serving Size: **155g**; Serves: **8**; Calories: **127**
Total Fat: **0g** Saturated Fat: **0g**; Trans Fat: **0g**
Protein: **2.1g**; Net Carbs: **27.8g**
Total Carbs: **30.9g**; Dietary Fiber: **3.1g**; Sugars: **24.5g**
Cholesterol: **0mg**; Sodium: **11mg**; Potassium: **24mg**;
Vitamin A: 280%; **Vitamin C**: 8%; **Calcium**: 4%; **Iron**: 4%.

Ingredients:
- 4 cups pumpkin puree
- ½ cup raw honey
- ¼ cup coconut palm sugar
- 1 teaspoon cinnamon
- 1 teaspoon pumpkin pie spice
- ¼ teaspoon sea salt
- 1/3 cup apple cider
- ¼ teaspoon lemon juice

Directions:
1. Put all ingredients into the slow cooker and cook on low for 6 hours, until thick.
2. You can store it in the refrigerator for up to 2 weeks.

Stuffed Apples

Prep Time: 10 minutes; Cook Time: 1 hours 30 minutes

Serving Size: **196g;** Serves: **5**; Calories: **248**

Total Fat: **7.2g** Saturated Fat: **2.8g;** Trans Fat: **0g**

Protein: **1.1g;** Net Carbs: **42g**

Total Carbs: **49.5g;** Dietary Fiber: **7.5g**; Sugars: **42g**

Cholesterol: **0mg;** Sodium: **0mg;** Potassium: **220mg;**

Vitamin A: 0%; **Vitamin C**: 55%; **Calcium**: 5%; **Iron**: 66%.

Ingredients:
- 5 apples, cored

For the filling
- 5 dried figs
- 1/3 cup maple syrup
- ¼ cup chopped pecans
- ¼ teaspoon salt
- ¼ teaspoon nutmeg
- 1 tablespoon fresh juice from a lemon
- 1 tablespoon coconut oil

For the water bath
- ½ cup water
- ½ teaspoon cinnamon

Directions:

1. In a medium bowl, stir together all the ingredients for the filling.
2. Remove the core from the apples and stuff them with the filling.
3. Pour the water bath into the slow cooker and place the stuffed apples into the bath.
4. Cook on high for 1.5 hours.

Power Bars

Prep Time: **10 minutes**; Cook Time: **8 hours**
Serving Size: **93g**; Serves: **6**; Calories: **373**
Total Fat: **22.4g** Saturated Fat: **2.9g**; Trans Fat: **0g**
Protein: **11.3g**; Net Carbs: **21.6g**
Total Carbs: **26.8g**; Dietary Fiber: **5.2g**; Sugars: **17.5g**
Cholesterol: **0mg**; Sodium: **4mg**; Potassium: **359mg**;
Vitamin A: 4%; **Vitamin C**: 1%; **Calcium**: 9%; **Iron**: 27%.

Ingredients:
- 1 cup whole almonds, toasted
- 1 cup pumpkin seeds, shelled
- 1 cup dried cranberries
- 1 cup chopped, pitted Medjool dates

Directions:
1. Wrap a 9×5-inch loaf pan with overhanging plastic.
2. Blend whole almonds in a food processor for about 4 minutes, until a ball starts to form.

3. Toss in the pumpkin seeds, dried cranberries and dates. Blend for 2 to 3 minutes more.
4. Transfer the dough into the loaf pan and press down firmly. Cover with plastic wrap and chill for about 1 hour.
5. When firm, remove from the pan and slice into bars.
6. You can store them in the refrigerator for up to 2 weeks.

Part 2

Introduction

The Paleo diet is a combination of carefully selected nutritious foods that are aimed at providing a healthy and desirable lifestyle. Its benefits are a notch higher as compared to other forms of diet in the society.

Anyone who has attempted to go on a diet must have realized how hectic it can be if one does not find 'the right food' that not only suits them but eventually provide fulfilling results. With the Paleo diet, you no longer have to worry about finding that custom made diet that works for you. This is because the Paleo diet has been proven to work for all individuals from all walks of life due to its unique capability to deal directly with a person's genetics.

Research indicates that modern diets, no matter how good they may appear to be, are the leading cause of degenerative diseases across the world. Unless one is fasting, a day will not go by without ingesting sugar, salt or fats. This has made many people in the society to wonder the maximum quantity for the body.

Paleo Slow Cooker

There is nothing as satisfying as a soft meal at the end of a long day. With pale, slow cooker recipes, even the toughest meals come out soft and tender. The pale, slow cooker has mouthwatering recipes that will leave your taste buds begging for more. Let's have a look at how some of the slow cooked meals are prepared.

Eggs and Breakfast

Veggie Spinach Omelette

Servings: 4
Prep Time: 10 minutes
Cook Time: **2 hours 10 minutes**
Ingredients:

- 1 cup spinach
- 4 eggs
- 1 cup broccoli florets
- 1 onion, chopped
- ½ tsp. sea salt
- 2 tomatoes, chopped

Directions:

1. Mix eggs and sea salt.
2. Add broccoli, tomatoes, spinach and chopped onion to the mixture, stir and pour in the slow cooker.
3. Cook for 2 hours.

Nutrition:

- Calories: 125

- Fat: 15 g
- Carbohydrates: 13 g
- Protein: 47 g

Butternut Squash N'Oatmeal

Servings: 2
Prep Time: 5 minutes
Cook Time: **8 hours**

Ingredients:

- 2 apples, cut
- 1 cup raw walnuts
- 1 tsp. cinnamon
  1 butternut squash, cut
  Directions:

1. **Put the walnuts into the combine or food processor and blend well.**
2. Mix the mixture and all remaining ingredients in the slow cooker. Cover and cook for 8 hours.

   Nutrition:

- Calories: 189
- Fat: 9 g
- Carbohydrates: 13 g
  Protein:15 g

Paleo Mexican Breakfast Casserole

Servings: 2
Prep Time: 5 minutes

Cook Time: **8 hours**
Ingredients:

- 8 eggs
- 200 g chopped mushrooms
- 4 slices bacon
- 1 chopped onion
- ½ tsp. sea salt
- ½ tsp. pepper
- Jalapeno and guacamole to serve

Directions:
1. <u>Firstly, fry bacon.</u>
2. Mix fried bacon, eggs, mushrooms. Onion, sea salt, pepper, and put in the slow cooker. Cover and cook for 6-8 hours.
3. Serve with jalapeno and guacamole.

Nutrition:
- Calories: 215
- Fat: 20 g
- Carbohydrates: 35 g
- Protein: 15 g

Mexican Casserole

Servings: 6
Prep Time: 5 minutes
Cook Time: **6 hours**

Ingredients:
- 2 chicken fillets, cut
- 1 onion, chopped

- 7-8 eggs whisked
- 300 g. mushrooms, chopped
- 1 red bell pepper, chopped
- ½ tsp. sea salt
  ½ tsp. black pepper
  Directions:
1. **Put fillets, onion, mushrooms, bell pepper in the slow cooker and pour eggs over. Season.**
2. Close and cook for 6 hours.
   Nutrition:
- Calories: 208
- Fat: 11 g
- Carbohydrates: 4 g
  Protein: 15.2g

Apple Cinnamon Oatmeal

Servings: 5
Prep Time: 5 minutes
Cook Time: **6 hours**

Ingredients:
- 2 sweet apples, peeled and chopped
- ½ tsp. cinnamon
- 1 tsp. brown sugar or honey
- 4 cups water
1 cup oats
Directions:

1. **Add all ingredients in the slow cooker. Stir.**
2. Cover and cook for 6 hours.

Nutrition:
- Calories: 130
- Fat: 1 g
- Carbohydrates: 27 g
Protein: 3 g

Blueberry Oatmeal

Servings: 8
Prep Time: 5 minutes

Cook Time: **4 hours**

Ingredients:

- 2 sweet apples, peeled and chopped
- ½ tsp. cinnamon
- 1 tsp. brown sugar or honey
- 4 cups water
- 1 cup fresh blueberries
1 cup oats
Directions:

1. **Add all ingredients in the slow cooker. Stir.**
2. Cover and cook for 4 hours.

Nutrition:

- Calories: 130
- Fat: 1 g
- Carbohydrates: 27 g
Protein: 3 g

Apple Quinoa with Cinnamon

Servings: 6
Prep Time: 5 minutes
Cook Time: **8 hours**

Ingredients:

- 2 tsp. cinnamon
- 1 tbsp. honey
- 1 cup quinoa
- 2 sweet apples, sliced
2 cups water
Directions:

1. **Put all ingredients in the slow cooker. Pour the water. Add the honey.**
2. Cover and cook for 8 hours.

   Nutrition:

- Calories: 220
- Fat: 2 g
- Carbohydrates: 30 g

Protein: 6 g

Chicken

Curry Chicken

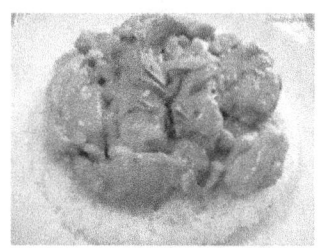

Servings: 9
Prep Time: 5 minutes
Cook Time: **4 hours**

Ingredients:
- 4 skinless chicken fillets
- 1 tsp. carry
- 1 tsp. paprika
- 1 tsp. sea salt
- 1 chopped onion
½ tsp. black pepper

Directions:
1. **Cut chicken fillets into quarters. Mix with carry, paprika, sea salt, pepper, add onion. Put in the slow cooker. Cover and cook for 4 hours.**
2. **Serve with tortillas.**

Nutrition:
- Calories: 116
- Fat: 4 g
- Carbohydrates: 16 g
Protein: 18 g

Polynesian Chicken

Servings: 6
Prep Time: 15 minutes
Cook Time: **3 hours**

Ingredients:

- 2 cups pineapple, quartered
- 4 chicken breasts, skinless, boneless cut into small pieces
- 2 minced cloves garlic
- 2 tbsp. honey
  2 tsp. fresh ginger
  Directions:

1. **Mix garlic, honey, ginger with pineapple juice.**
2. Place chicken and pineapple in the slow cooker.
3. **Pour the mixture over the chicken and pineapple. Cover and cook for 3 hours.**

Nutrition:
- Calories: 255
- Fat: 7 g
- Carbohydrates: 31 g
Protein: 18 g

Balsamic Mushroom and Chicken

Servings: 8
Prep Time: 10 minutes
Cook Time: **4 hours**

Ingredients:
- 1 chopped onion
- 1 tsp. salt
- 1 tbsp. balsamic vinegar

- 200 g mushrooms
- 1 cup low-fat yogurt
- ½ tsp. black pepper
- 1 minced garlic clove
  4 chicken fillets, sliced
  Directions:

1. **Put the chicken fillets in the slow cooker. Place over the fillets onion, mushrooms, garlic, and balsamic vinegar.**
2. **Season with salt and black pepper.**
3. **Cover and cook for 4 hours. At the end pour the yogurt and stir well.**

   Nutrition:

- Calories: 187
- Fat: 4 g
- Carbohydrates: 9 g
  Protein: 27 g

Healthy Chicken Yakitori

Servings: 6

Prep Time: 5 minutes
Cook Time: **2 hours**

Ingredients:

- 1 pound chicken breast, diced
- 1 tbsp dry sherry
- 1 tsp minced ginger
- 1 tsp vegetable oil
  2 cloves garlic, minced
  Directions:

1. **Add the chicken breast, dry sherry, ginger and garlic in the slow cooker.**
2. Stir well and cook for 2 hours.

   Nutrition:

- Calories: 186
- Fat: 4 g
- Carbohydrates: 17 g
  Protein: 15 g

Tasty Chicken Fillets

Servings: 4
Prep Time: 15 minutes
Cook Time: **4 hours**

Ingredients:

- 4 chicken fillets
- 1 tsp. sea salt
- ½ tsp. black pepper
- ½ tsp. paprika
- 1 onion, chopped
  1 cup water
  Directions:

1. **Add all ingredients in the slow cooker. Pour the water.**
2. Cover and cook for 4 hours.

    Nutrition:

- Calories: 130
- Fat: 3 g
- Carbohydrates: 18 g
  Protein: 60 g

Southwest Chicken

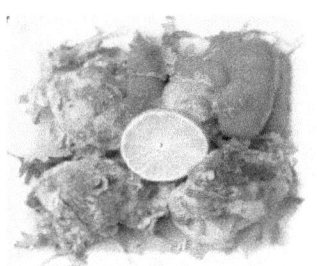

Servings: 6
Prep Time: 5 minutes

Cook Time: **6 hours**
Ingredients:

- 6 chicken breast
- 2 red bell peppers
- 1 tsp. cumin
- 1 tsp. paprika
- 1 tsp. sea salt
- 1 tsp. coriander
- ½ tsp. black pepper
- 1 onion, chopped
- 1 lime, quartered
- 2 cloves garlic, minced
- 5 cups water

Directions:

1. Add all ingredients in the slow cooker. Pour the water.
2. Cover and cook for 6 hours.

Nutrition:

- Calories: 256

- Fat: 5 g
- Carbohydrates: 23 g
- Protein: 22 g

Honey Chicken

Servings: 6
Prep Time: 5 minutes
Cook Time: **4 hours**

Ingredients:

- 1 lb. chicken wings
- 2 tbsp. olive oil
- 2 cloves garlic, minced
- 4 tbsp. honey
  1 tsp. sea salt
  Directions:

1. **Mix wings with the honey. Put in the slow cooker. Season**
2. Cover and cook for 4 hours.

   Nutrition:

- Calories: 141
- Fat: 4 g
- Carbohydrates: 31 g
  Protein: 35 g

Chicken Broths

Servings: 4
Prep Time: 5 minutes
Cook Time: **6 hours**

Ingredients:

- 8 chicken broths
- 1 tsp. sea salt
- ½ tsp. black pepper
  ½ tsp. paprika
  Directions:

1. Add all ingredients in the slow cooker.
2. Cover and cook for 6 hours.

   Nutrition:

- Calories: 219
- Fat: 4 g
- Carbohydrates: 17 g
  Protein: 26 g

Beef

Salsa Verde Beef

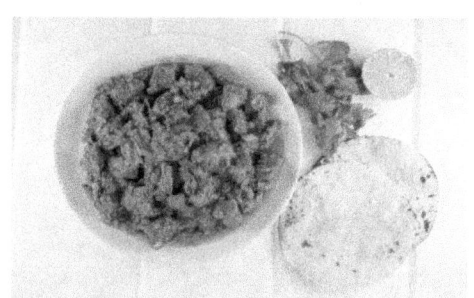

Servings: 6
Prep Time: 5 minutes
Cook Time: **8 hours**

Ingredients:

- 2 tbsp. salsa verde
- 1 chopped onion
- 2 kg. lean beef eye round, chunked
- ½ tsp. salt
- ½ tsp. oregano
- ½ tsp. black pepper
- 2 minced garlic cloves
  ½ tsp. cumin
  Directions:

1. **Mix all ingredients in the slow cooker.**
2. Cover and cook for 8 hours.

Nutrition:
- Calories: 226
- Fat: 5 g
- Carbohydrates: 7 g
Protein: 35 g

Beef Machaca

Servings: 8
Prep Time: 10 minutes
Cook Time: **8 hours**

Ingredients:
- 4 beef roasts
- 3 tbsp. lime juice
- 1 tsp. sea salt
- 2 minced garlic cloves
- ½ tbsp. oregano
- ½ tsp. black pepper
3 cups chopped tomatoes

Directions:

1. **Put beef roast, lime juice, garlic, oregano, chopped tomatoes in the slow cooker. Season with sea salt and pepper.**
2. Cover and cook for 8 hours.

   Nutrition:

- Calories: 247
- Fat: 6 g
- Carbohydrates: 6 g
  Protein: 40 g

Balsamic Beef

Servings: 4
Prep Time: 15 minutes
Cook Time: **7 hours**

Ingredients:

- 1 kg beef cubed
- 1 chopped onion
- 3 minced gloves garlic

- 4 carrots
- 1 cup water
- 1 tbsp. chopped thyme
- 1 tsp. sea salt
  ½ tsp. black pepper
  Directions:

1. **Cut the beef and carrots into large chunks.**
2. Put in the slow cooker. Add all remaining ingredients. Pour water.
3. **Cover and cook for 7 hours.**

   Nutrition:

- Calories: 199
- Fat: 5 g
- Carbohydrates: 6 g
  Protein: 16 g

Chorizo Spiced Pulled Beef

Servings: 6

Prep Time: 10 minutes
Cook Time: **4 hours**

Ingredients:

- 1 kg beef tenderloin
- 2 tsp. paprika
- 1 tsp. chili pepper
- 1 tsp. oregano
- ½ tsp. coriander
- 1 tsp. Sea salt
  ½ tsp. black pepper
  Directions:

1. **Mix all ingredients in the slow cooker.**
2. Cover and cook for 4 hours.

    Nutrition:

- Calories: 190
- Fat: 4 g
- Carbohydrates: 5 g
  Protein: 33 g

Beef with Vegetables

Servings: 6
Prep Time: 10 minutes

Cook Time: **8 hours**
Ingredients:

- 5 carrots, chopped
- 2 cloves garlic, minced
- 2 cups water
- 1 onion, chopped
- 2 celeries, chopped
- 800 g beef, cut
- 1 tsp. sea salt
- 1 tsp. paprika
- ½ tsp. black pepper

Directions:

1. <u>Mix all spices. Cover the beef with spices.</u>
2. Put vegetables and beef in the slow cooker. Pour the water.
3. Cover and cook for 8 hours.

Nutrition:

- Calories: 273
- Fat: 13 g
- Carbohydrates: 8 g
- Protein: 21 g

Beef with Vegetables

Servings: 4
Prep Time: 5 minutes
Cook Time: **8 hours**

Ingredients:

- 1 kg beef stew meat, cut into pieces
- 3 carrots, chopped
- 1 celery, chopped
- 2 onions, sliced
- 1 cabbage, chopped
- 2 cloves garlic, minced
- 1 tsp. sea salt
- ½ tsp. black pepper
- 1 tsp. paprika
  2 cups water
  Directions:

1. Add all ingredients in the slow cooker. Mix well.
2. Cover and cook for 6 hours.
   Nutrition:

- Calories: 245

- Fat: 20 g
- Carbohydrates: 14 g
  Protein: 38 g

Beef with Broccoli

Servings: 4
Prep Time: 5 minutes
Cook Time: **4 hours**

Ingredients:

- 1 kg beef, sliced
- 2 cloves garlic, minced
- 4 cups broccoli, chopped
- 1 onion, chopped
- 1 tsp. sea salt
- ½ tsp. black pepper
  4 cups water
  Directions:

1. Add all ingredients in the slow cooker. Pour the water. Stir well.
2. Cover and cook for 4 hours.

   Nutrition:
- Calories: 278
- Fat: 19 g
- Carbohydrates: 16 g
  Protein: 31 g

Mushrooms

Herb Mushrooms

Servings: 4
Prep Time: 20 minutes

Cook Time: **4 hours**
Ingredients:
- 3 minced garlic cloves

- 2 bay leaves
- 300 g mushrooms
- ½ tsp. oregano
- ½ tsp. basil
- ½ tsp. salt
- 1 cup coconut milk
- ½ tsp. black pepper

Directions:

1. Put all ingredients, except milk, in the slow cooker. Cover and cook for 4 hours.
2. When is cooked, add milk and cover. Let stand for 10 minutes. Serve!

Nutrition:

- Calories: 106
- Fat: 10 g
- Carbohydrates: 6 g
- Protein: 5 g

Potato with Mushrooms

Servings: 6
Prep Time: 10 minutes
Cook Time: **3 hours**

Ingredients:

- 10 potatoes, peeled and quartered
- 1 carrot, peeled and quartered
- 300 g mushrooms, quartered
- 1 tsp. salt
- 1tsp. black pepper
½ tsp. fresh oregano
Directions:

1. **Put all ingredients to the slow cooker.**
2. Cover and cook for 3 hours.

   Nutrition:

- Calories: 234
- Fat: 5 g
- Carbohydrates: 15 g
Protein: 9 g

Rosemary Mushrooms

Servings: 4
Prep Time: 5 minutes
Cook Time: **2 hours**

Ingredients:

- 1 tbsp. olive oil
- 1 kg quartered mushrooms
- 2 tbsp. chopped fresh rosemary
- 1 tsp. sea salt
½ tsp. black pepper
Directions:

1. **Add all listed above ingredients to the slow cooker, stir well.**
2. Cover and cook for 2 hours.

Nutrition:

- Calories: 86
- Fat: 7 g
- Carbohydrates: 5 g
Protein: 4 g

Soups and Stews

Pumpkin Soup

Servings: 10
Prep Time: 15 minutes
Cook Time: **4 hours**

Ingredients:

- 1 peeled and diced sweet apple
- 1 middle pumpkin, cut into small pieces
- 1 chopped onion
- 1 tsp. pumpkin spice
- 3 cups chicken stock
- 1 tsp. sea salt
- 1 tsp. black pepper
- 1 tsp. paprika
  2 cups water
  Directions:

1. **Put apple, pumpkin, onion, chicken stock in the slow cooker. Cover and cook for 4 hours.**
2. Meanwhile blend pumpkin spice, paprika, sea salt, and pepper. Add to the slow cooker and blend one more time using a hand blender.

Nutrition:

- Calories: 66
- Fat: 2 g
- Carbohydrates: 11 g
Protein: 4 g

Fiesta Chicken Stew

Servings: 10
Prep Time: 5 minutes

Cook Time: **8 hours**
Ingredients:

- 1 minced clove garlic
- 2 cups black beans

- 1 chopped onion
- 1 cup green chili pepper
- 1 cup fresh corn
- 1 tsp. pepper
- 1 tsp. cumin
- 1 tsp. salt
- 2 tbsp. fresh cilantro
- 3 cups fat-free chicken broth
- 2 chicken fillets, cut into small pieces
- 1 tbsp. lime juice

Directions:
1. Mix all ingredients in the slow cooker.
2. Cover and cook for 8 hours.

Nutrition:
- Calories: 192
- Fat: 3 g
- Carbohydrates: 21 g
- Protein: 20 g

Chicken Soup

Servings: 8
Prep Time: 5 minutes
Cook Time: **6 hours**

Ingredients:

- 3 sliced carrots
- 1 chopped onion
- ½ tsp. black pepper
- 1 tsp. sea salt
- 4 cups water
- 3 chopped celery
500 g chicken fillets, sliced
Directions:

1. **Add to the slow cooker carrots, black pepper, onion, sea salt, celery, and chicken fillets.**
2. Cover and cook for 6 hours.

   Nutrition:

- Calories: 180
- Fat: 5 g
- Carbohydrates: 10 g
Protein: 17 g

Cream of Chicken and Rice Soup

Servings: 8
Prep Time: 5 minutes
Cook Time: 8 hours 15 minutes

Ingredients:

- 3 sliced carrots
- 2 chopped cloves garlic
- 1 cubed potato
- ½ tsp. red pepper
- 1 chopped onion
- ½ tsp. black pepper
- 1 tsp. salt
- 1 chopped celery
- 1 cup low-fat milk
- 500 g chicken fillets, sliced
  1 cup rice
  Directions:

1. **Add to the slow cooker carrots, garlic, potato, red and black pepper, onion, salt, celery, rice, and chicken fillets. Cover and cook for 8 hours.**
2. When cooked add milk, stir well. Cover and cook for 15 minutes.

Nutrition:
- Calories: 180
- Fat: 5 g
- Carbohydrates: 10 g
- Protein: 17 g

Beef and Pepper Stew

Servings: 4
Prep Time: 15 minutes

Cook Time: **6 hours**
Ingredients:

- 600 g beef meat, cut
- 4 peppers, cut
- 1 tsp. sea salt
- 1 tbsp. olive oil
- 2 carrots, sliced
- 1 onion, chopped
- 3 tomatoes, chopped
- 2 cloves garlic, minced
- 5 cups water
- ½ tsp. black pepper

Directions:

1. Put all ingredients in the slow cooker. Pour the water.
2. Cover and cook for 6 hours.

Nutrition:

- Calories: 141
- Fat: 4 g
- Carbohydrates: 21 g
- Protein: 7 g

Spinach Chicken Soup

Servings: 8
Prep Time: 5 minutes
Cook Time: **4 hours**

Ingredients:

- 1 celery, chopped
- 1 onion, chopped
- 2 carrots, chopped
- 2 cups spinach
- 3 chicken fillets. Sliced
- 2 tomatoes, chopped
- 1 tsp. sea salt
- ½ tsp. black pepper
- ½ tsp. thyme

10 cups water
Directions:

1. **Add all ingredients to the slow cooker. Season and pour water.**
2. Cover and cook for 4 hours.

   Nutrition:
- Calories: 123
- Fat: 16 g
- Carbohydrates: 24 g
- Protein: 28 g

Pumpkin Chicken Soup

Servings: 6
Prep Time: 5 minutes
Cook Time: **6 hours**

Ingredients:

- 2 chicken fillets, sliced
- 700 g. pumpkin quartered
- 1 celery, chopped
- 2 onions, chopped
- 3 carrots, chopped
- 1 tsp. sea salt
- ½ black pepper
10 cups water
Directions:

1. **Mix all ingredients in the slow cooker. Stir.**
2. Cover and cook for 6 hours. When is done, blend well using a blender.

Nutrition:

- Calories: 240
- Fat: 19 g
- Carbohydrates: 28 g

Protein: 36 g

Beef and Vegetables Stew

Servings: 6
Prep Time: 5 minutes
Cook Time: **8 hours**

Ingredients:

- 400 g beef, cut into pieces
- 1 onion, sliced
- 2 carrots, quartered
- 2 celeries, quartered
- 300 g. mushrooms, sliced
- 1 tsp. sea salt
- ½ tsp. black pepper
  5 cups water
  Directions:

1. **Add all ingredients to the slow cooker. Season.**
2. Cover and cook for 8 hours.

   Nutrition:

- Calories: 267

- Fat: 20 g
- Carbohydrates: 37 g
  Protein: 32 g

www.ingramcontent.com/pod-product-compliance
Lightning Source LLC
Chambersburg PA
CBHW071440070526
44578CB00001B/170